D1544203

The Mind
Has Cliffs
of Fall

ALSO BY ROBERT PINSKY

POETRY

At the Foundling Hospital
Selected Poems
Gulf Music
Jersey Rain
The Figured Wheel
The Want Bone
History of My Heart
An Explanation of America
Sadness and Happiness
The Inferno of Dante (translation)

PROSE

Thousands of Broadways
The Life of David
Democracy, Culture and the Voice of Poetry
The Sounds of Poetry
Poetry and the World
The Situation of Poetry
Landor's Poetry

EDITED BY ROBERT PINSKY

Singing School
Essential Pleasures
An Invitation to Poetry
Poems to Read
Americans' Favorite Poems
Handbook of Heartbreak

The Mind Has Cliffs of Fall

POEMS AT THE EXTREMES OF FEELING

EDITED BY Robert Pinsky

W. W. NORTON & COMPANY
Independent Publishers Since 1923

Since this page cannot legibly accommodate all the copyright notices,
pages 217–23 constitute an extension of the copyright page.

For information about special discounts for bulk purchases, please contact
W. W. Norton Special Sales at specialsales@wwnorton.com or 800-233-4830

Manufacturing by Lake Book Manufacturing
Book design by Brooke Koven
Production manager: Julia Druskin

Library of Congress Cataloging-in-Publication Data

Names: Pinsky, Robert editor.
Title: The mind has cliffs of fall : poems at the extremes
of feeling / edited by Robert Pinsky.
Description: First edition. | New York ; London :
W. W. Norton & Company, 2019. | Includes index.
Identifiers: LCCN 2019021534 | ISBN 9781324001782 (hardcover)
Subjects: LCSH: Emotions—Poetry.
Classification: LCC PN6110.E5 M56 2019 | DDC 808.81/9353—dc23
LC record available at https://lccn.loc.gov/2019021534

W. W. Norton & Company, Inc., 500 Fifth Avenue, New York, N.Y. 10110
www.wwnorton.com

W. W. Norton & Company Ltd., 15 Carlisle Street, London W1D 3BS

1 2 3 4 5 6 7 8 9 0

To Margaret, Benjamin, Rosalind, Lillian,
Hazel, Simon, Elliot, and Sam

CONTENTS

———

Grief

Love and Rage

Despair

Guilt, Shame, Blame

Manic Laughter

INTRODUCTION

No worst, there is none. Pitched past pitch of grief,
More pangs will, schooled at forepangs, wilder wring.
Comforter, where, where is your comforting?

No worst, there is none. With that assertion, in words of one syllable,
Gerard Manley Hopkins begins the sonnet that strikes a keynote for
this anthology. The ninth line provides the words paraphrased for this
book's title:

O the mind, mind has mountains; cliffs of fall
Frightful, sheer, no-man-fathomed.

There is absolutely nothing worse than these cliffs of fall, he says.
They are in the mind, which makes them more inescapably real and
more urgent, not less. And absolutely no one can fathom them. In
the poem's concluding line, even comfort—comfort itself!—is nearly
as terrifying as the cliffs:

Here! creep,
Wretch, under a comfort serves in a whirlwind: all
Life death does end and each day dies with sleep.

No and *all* and *each*: the simplicity of the terms emphasizes the total
quality of the feeling.

Emily Dickinson, too, with her characteristic imaginative force, begins a poem with a large, startling assertion: "I felt a Funeral, in my Brain." And like Hopkins she deploys the word "all" with absolute, weird authority:

> Then Space—began to toll,
> As all the Heavens were a Bell

These are examples of the quality that defines this book: emotion at the extremes.

But isn't *all* poetry at the extremes of feeling?

A reasonable question. However, I think not. In art as in life, there are matters of degree or scale. In choosing poems to include I have sought what I feel in Hopkins' "no-man-fathomed" cliffs and Dickinson's Space tolling the bell of "all the Heavens": immensity. Not just the Heavens, but *all* the Heavens.

In contrast, a friend of mine said about a respected contemporary poet: "He writes very well about his little feelings." In other words, my friend finds those poems limited in scope, but not necessarily worthless.

Certainly, personal feelings—for example, unhappiness in one's love life—may seem small to others, but in poetry it all depends upon how you do it. Fulke Greville (1554–1628) compares disappointment in love to doomsday:

> When all this All doth pass from age to age,
> And revolution in a circle turn,
> Then heavenly justice doth appear like rage,
> The caves do roar, the very seas do burn,
>   Glory grows dark, the sun becomes a night,
>   And makes this great world feel a greater might. (p. 85)

He does not seem to mean this analogy as a mere comic exaggeration; he feels truly mistreated: colossally so. But at the same time, along with what I'll call sincere hyperbole, Greville conveys an awareness that he is ranting far beyond normal, rational boundaries. His images of the Last Judgment are on a cosmic scale—an "All" with a capital *A*.

His transition to the personal, through a series of abstractions, is equally violent and total: "Grace is diseas'd," he continues, and "desire must be wise, / And look more ways than one, or lose her eyes." Then, in a move that characterizes many poems I love in this anthology, a deliberate anticlimax:

> My age of joy is past, of woe begun,
> Absence my presence is, strangeness my grace,
> With them that walk against me, is my sun:
> The wheel is turn'd, I hold the lowest place,
>   What can be good to me since my love is
>   To do me harm, content to do amiss?

The poem's concluding line, with its "harm" and "to do amiss," is comically mild, but with a self-diagnostic candor that underscores the out-of-control feeling.

Allen Ginsberg (1926–1997) in a similar spirit takes the personal far beyond its normal dimensions. Citing his predecessor Christopher Smart, Ginsberg writes:

> A flower in my head
>   Has fallen through my eye;
> Someday I'll be dead:
>   I love the Lord on high,
>   I wish He'd pull my daisy.
>   Smart went crazy,
>   Smart went crazy. (p. 194)

Does the line "I wish He'd pull my daisy" indicate Ginsberg's readiness for God to harvest him from life? Or his wish for a sexual favor from God? Death? Or orgasm? I think the answer has to be *all of the above*, echoing the large, encompassing word deployed by Greville, Dickinson, and Hopkins.

As these quotations illustrate, there are poems that not only enter the terrain of psychotherapy, but transform the psyche's topography and its climate. That transformation, the never-defined central quality of art, incorporates lament and celebration, or indictment and exaltation, ridicule and reverence. That dance of contradictions bears some resemblance to what psychology means by the term "bipolar"—except that the manic and depressive do not merely alternate, but may be simultaneous. An example is the explicit despair and the implicit, *formal* elation of William Cowper (1731–1800):

LINES WRITTEN DURING A PERIOD OF INSANITY

Hatred and vengeance, my eternal portion,
Scarce can endure delay of execution,
Wait, with impatient readiness, to seize my
                    Soul in a moment.

Damn'd below Judas: more abhorr'd than he was,
Who for a few pence sold his holy Master.
Twice betrayed Jesus me, the last delinquent,
                    Deems the profanest.

Man disavows, and Deity disowns me:
Hell might afford my miseries a shelter;
Therefore hell keeps her ever hungry mouths all
                    Bolted against me.

Hard lot! encompass'd with a thousand dangers;
Weary, faint, trembling with a thousand terrors;
I'm called, if vanquish'd, to receive a sentence
                    Worse than Abiram's.

Him the vindictive rod of angry justice
Sent quick and howling to the centre headlong;
I, fed with judgment, in a fleshly tomb, am
                    Buried above ground.

Damned below Judas, condemned with a sentence worse than Abiram's (who went to hell alive), exiled from hell itself, the poet writes with manic energy in the demanding, forward-tumbling meter of the Sapphic stanza. The adjectives "weary" and "faint" appear in a dynamic line, with the vibrant "trembling with a thousand terrors." To say that there is no worst can be, in this inward realm, kind of triumphant: a contradiction between matter and music, distress and art, as in the poem's title and in its volcanic rhythms.

But the extremes of emotion are themselves capacious, various, and inclusive. I try to indicate that scope with the section titles: "The Sleep of Reason," "Grief," "Love and Rage," "Despair," "Guilt, Shame, Blame," and "Manic Laughter." As the last category suggests, extremes and immensities are not necessarily solemn. The epigrammatic hauteur of Louise Bogan (1897–1970) has the kind of sweeping force that I've made my editorial standard:

SEVERAL VOICES OUT OF A CLOUD

> Come, drunks and drug-takers; come, perverts unnerved!
> Receive the laurel, given, though late, on merit; to whom
>   and wherever deserved.
>
> Parochial punks, trimmers, nice people, joiners true-blue,
> Get the hell out of the way of the laurel. It is deathless
>   And it isn't for you.

Without the literal "all," the poet clearly speaks with all-encompassing, absolute conviction. The Swiftian list-twister "nice people" expands the scornful gaze, and so does the implicit empathy of "unnerved." Above all, she celebrates that "merit" absolutely, uncompromisingly *rules*. I hear a social-class note in that celebration—in a way, it is an antisocial note. Bogan grew up in a disorderly and disreputable working-class family, dropped out of Boston University in her freshman year . . . and after some years, on her merits, became the poetry critic for *The New Yorker*.

The section that includes Bogan's "Several Voices Out of a Cloud" begins with John Wilmot's hero-deflating "Grecian Kindness" (p. 179) and ends with recent poems by C. Dale Young, Kathryn Maris, Jill McDonough, Natalie Shapero, and Katie Willingham. I hope that the historical arrangement of each section, from quite early poems to contemporaries, will add another kind of interest, tracing similarities from Anonymous (p. 3) to Graham Barnhart (p. 30); from Fulke Greville (p. 35) to Jenny George (p. 80); from Sappho (p. 83) to Keetje Kuipers (p. 118); from Dante Alighieri (p. 121) to Rowan Ricardo Phillips (p. 148); from Anonymous (p. 151) to Adam Day (p. 176).

Poetry is the most intimate art: its medium is each reader's imagined or actual voice. A poem gets under your skin, and invites your breath. Its theater is the part of the brain linked to the organs of speech, the core in language of our need for other people. I've tried to supply a glimpse into that place where art engages the largest, yet most inward, experiences of each unique life.

THE
SLEEP
OF
REASON

Anonymous, "The Man of Double Deed"

THIS POEM exemplifies how poetry can join reason and unreason, method and wildness, so effectively that the opposites become part of a single process. The links and repetitions seem governed partly by rhyme and partly by some obsessive, hyper-rational formula of causality. As in dreams or some forms of mental illness, the systematic becomes a form of derangement.

The Man of Double Deed

There was a man of double deed,
Who sowed his garden full of seed;
When the seed began to grow,
'Twas like a garden full of snow;
When the snow began to melt,
'Twas like a ship without a belt;
When the ship began to sail,
'Twas like a bird without a tail;
When the bird began to fly,
'Twas like an eagle in the sky;
When the sky began to roar,
'Twas like a lion at my door;
When my door began to crack,
'Twas like a stick across my back;
When my back began to smart,
'Twas like a penknife in my heart;
And when my heart began to bleed,
'Twas death, and death, and death indeed.

Fulke Greville (1554–1628), "In Night, When Colors All to Black Are Cast"

A **VIVID** and reasonable diagnostic explanation.

In Night, When Colors All to Black Are Cast

In night, when colors all to black are cast,
Distinction lost, or gone down with the light,
The eye, a watch to inward senses placed,
Not seeing, yet still having power of sight,

Gives vain alarums to the inward sense,
Where fear, stirred up with witty tyranny,
Confounds all powers, and through self-offence
Doth forge and raise impossibility,

Such as in thick depriving darknesses
Proper reflections of the error be,
And images of self-confusednesses,
Which hurt imaginations only see:—
    And from this nothing seen, tells news of devils,
    Which but expressions be of inward evils.

William Cowper (1731–1800), "Lines Written During a Period of Insanity"

PAIN AND conviction. The energy of the writing, the perfection of form, recall the modern notion of "bipolar" mental illness. Here, mania and despair are simultaneous.

Lines Written During a Period of Insanity

Hatred and vengeance, my eternal portion,
Scarce can endure delay of execution,
Wait, with impatient readiness, to seize my
                Soul in a moment.

Damn'd below Judas: more abhorr'd than he was,
Who for a few pence sold his holy Master.
Twice betrayed Jesus me, the last delinquent,
                Deems the profanest.

Man disavows, and Deity disowns me:
Hell might afford my miseries a shelter;
Therefore hell keeps her ever hungry mouths all
                Bolted against me.

Hard lot! encompass'd with a thousand dangers;
Weary, faint, trembling with a thousand terrors;
I'm called, if vanquish'd, to receive a sentence
                Worse than Abiram's.

Him the vindictive rod of angry justice
Sent quick and howling to the centre headlong;
I, fed with judgment, in a fleshly tomb, am
                Buried above ground.

Emily Dickinson (1830–1886), "I Felt a Funeral, in My Brain" (no. 280)

A POET with unique access to the quality of reason above reason.

280

I felt a Funeral, in my Brain,
And Mourners to and fro
Kept treading—treading—till it seemed
That Sense was breaking through—

And when they all were seated,
A Service, like a Drum—
Kept beating—beating—till I thought
My Mind was going numb—

And then I heard them lift a Box
And creak across my Soul
With those same Boots of Lead, again,
Then Space—began to toll,

As all the Heavens were a Bell,
And Being, but an Ear,
And I, and Silence, some strange Race
Wrecked, solitary, here—

And then a Plank in Reason, broke,
And I dropped down, and down—
And hit a World, at every plunge,
And Finished knowing—then—

Hart Crane (1889–1932), "To Brooklyn Bridge"

THE HYPERBOLIC, outpacing curve of pure, creative aspiration. Beyond reason in its nature.

To Brooklyn Bridge

How many dawns, chill from his rippling rest
The seagull's wings shall dip and pivot him,
Shedding white rings of tumult, building high
Over the chained bay waters Liberty—

Then, with inviolate curve, forsake our eyes
As apparitional as sails that cross
Some page of figures to be filed away;
—Till elevators drop us from our day . . .

I think of cinemas, panoramic sleights
With multitudes bent toward some flashing scene
Never disclosed, but hastened to again,
Foretold to other eyes on the same screen;

And Thee, across the harbor, silver-paced
As though the sun took step of thee, yet left
Some motion ever unspent in thy stride—
Implicitly thy freedom staying thee!

Out of some subway scuttle, cell or loft
A bedlamite speeds to thy parapets,
Tilting there momently, shrill shirt ballooning,
A jest falls from the speechless caravan.

Down Wall, from girder into street noon leaks,
A rip-tooth of the sky's acetylene,
All afternoon the cloud-flown derricks turn . . .
Thy cables breathe the North Atlantic still.

And obscure as that heaven of the Jews,
Thy guerdon . . . Accolade thou dost bestow
Of anonymity time cannot raise:
Vibrant reprieve and pardon thou dost show.

O harp and altar, of the fury fused,
(How could mere toil align thy choiring strings!)
Terrific threshold of the prophet's pledge,
Prayer of pariah, and the lover's cry—

Again the traffic lights that skim thy swift
Unfractioned idiom, immaculate sigh of stars,
Beading thy path—condense eternity:
And we have seen night lifted in thine arms.

Under thy shadow by the piers I waited;
Only in darkness is thy shadow clear.
The City's fiery parcels all undone,
Already snow submerges an iron year . . .

O Sleepless as the river under thee,
Vaulting the sea, the prairies' dreaming sod,
Unto us lowliest sometime sweep, descend
And of the curveship lend a myth to God.

George Oppen (1908–1984), from *Of Being Numerous*

OPPEN REFLECTS on the unreasoning reasons of war, on "Failure and the guilt / Of failure"—all embedded in us, fatally. We "might half-hope," he says, for forgiveness or even mere irrelevance. He refers to Thomas Hardy's poem "The Oxen." The word "hope" appears also in Hardy's "The Darkling Thrush" (p. 131).

from Of Being Numerous

—They await

War, and the news
Is war

As always

That the juices may flow in them
Tho the juices lie.

Great things have happened
On the earth and given it history, armies
And the ragged hordes moving and the passions
Of that death. But who escapes
Death

Among these riders
Of the subway,

They know
By now as I know

Failure and the guilt
Of failure.
As in Hardy's poem of Christmas

We might half-hope to find the animals
In the sheds of a nation
Kneeling at midnight,

Farm animals,
Draft animals, beasts for slaughter
Because it would mean they have forgiven us,
Or which is the same thing,
That we do not altogether matter.

Elizabeth Bishop (1911–1979), "Visits to St. Elizabeths"

AS WITH "The Man of Double Deed" (p. 3), formal imagination entering the darkness, powered by the mighty, quasi-rational engine of a system.

Visits to St. Elizabeths

1950

This is the house of Bedlam.

This is the man
that lies in the house of Bedlam.

This is the time
of the tragic man
that lies in the house of Bedlam.

This is a wristwatch
telling the time
of the talkative man
that lies in the house of Bedlam.

This is a sailor
wearing the watch
that tells the time
of the honored man
that lies in the house of Bedlam.

This is the roadstead all of board
reached by the sailor

wearing the watch
that tells the time
of the old, brave man
that lies in the house of Bedlam.

These are the years and the walls of the ward,
the winds and clouds of the sea of board
sailed by the sailor
wearing the watch
that tells the time
of the cranky man
that lies in the house of Bedlam.

This is a Jew in a newspaper hat
that dances weeping down the ward
over the creaking sea of board
beyond the sailor
winding his watch
that tells the time
of the cruel man
that lies in the house of Bedlam.

This is a world of books gone flat.
This is a Jew in a newspaper hat
that dances weeping down the ward
over the creaking sea of board
of the batty sailor
that winds his watch
that tells the time
of the busy man
that lies in the house of Bedlam.

This is a boy that pats the floor
to see if the world is there, is flat,
for the widowed Jew in the newspaper hat
that dances weeping down the ward

waltzing the length of a weaving board
by the silent sailor
that hears his watch
that ticks the time
of the tedious man
that lies in the house of Bedlam.

These are the years and the walls and the door
that shut on a boy that pats the floor
to feel if the world is there and flat.
This is a Jew in a newspaper hat
that dances joyfully down the ward
into the parting seas of board
past the staring sailor
that shakes his watch
that tells the time
of the poet, the man
that lies in the house of Bedlam.

This is the soldier home from the war.
These are the years and the walls and the door
that shut on a boy that pats the floor
to see if the world is round or flat.
This is a Jew in a newspaper hat
that dances carefully down the ward,
walking the plank of a coffin board
with the crazy sailor
that shows his watch
that tells the time
of the wretched man
that lies in the house of Bedlam.

Czeslaw Milosz (1911–2004), "Bypassing Rue Descartes," translated by Renata Gorczynski and Robert Hass

"ABOLISHED CUSTOMS" versus "the universal, beautiful ideas" . . . that historical moment when, the poet says, "I entered the universal" perceived from the future, or even as though from the underworld. And as the street name of the title implies, in defense of reason, as well as custom? René Descartes, as well as the taboo against killing the harmless creature?

Bypassing Rue Descartes

I descended toward the Seine, shy, a traveler,
A young barbarian just come to the capital of the world.

We were many, from Jassy and Koloshvar, Wilno and Bucharest,
   Saigon and Marrakesh,
Ashamed to remember the customs of our homes,
About which nobody here should ever be told:
The clapping for servants, barefooted girls hurry in,
Dividing food with incantations,
Choral prayers recited by master and household together.

I had left the cloudy provinces behind,
I entered the universal, dazzled and desiring.

Soon enough, many from Jassy and Koloshvar, or Saigon or
   Marrakesh
Would be killed because they wanted to abolish the customs of
   their homes.

Soon enough, their peers were seizing power
In order to kill in the name of the universal, beautiful ideas.

Meanwhile the city behaved in accordance with its nature,
Rustling with throaty laughter in the dark,
Baking long breads and pouring wine into clay pitchers,
Buying fish, lemons, and garlic at street markets,
Indifferent as it was to honor and shame and greatness and glory,
Because that had been done already and had transformed itself
Into monuments representing nobody knows whom,
Into arias hardly audible and into turns of speech.

Again I lean on the rough granite of the embankment,
As if I had returned from travels through the underworlds
And suddenly saw in the light the reeling wheel of the seasons
Where empires have fallen and those once living are now dead.

There is no capital of the world, neither here nor anywhere else,
And the abolished customs are restored to their small fame
And now I know that the time of human generations is not like the
    time of the earth.

As to my heavy sins, I remember one most vividly:
How, one day, walking on a forest path along a stream,
I pushed a rock down onto a water snake coiled in the grass.

And what I have met with in life was the just punishment
Which reaches, sooner or later, the breaker of a taboo.

Tom Sleigh (b. 1953), "Block and Bag"

THE POWER of what Freudian professionals call "projection." And as part of projection, the urge to take (and create) sides.

Block and Bag

Pursuit, delay, anxious moments of dallying,
then leaps, bounds, hilarious cartwheels turning
manic with rage or fear performed in a concrete

courtyard bare but for hotel windows replicating
everywhere these mad, senseless, random chases,
a little styrofoam block fiery as Achilles

racing after a plastic bag kiting and billowing
round and round this blah arena, this angle/plane world
stripped to extremes of sun scraping concrete

bare, or blasted dark, obliviated by clouds,
the light neutered to the spirit's dullest grays while Block
and Bag now seem hunter/prey, john/whore,

then inexplicably bound and flutter to a halt,
exhausted, Block's corners pitted, rounded
by bumps and skids and somersaults,

Bag blowzy and worn, bedraggled by all this
unexpected passion, this afflatus of breath swelling
it full then sucked out so it collapses in ruin,

abject, pleading, overdoing it maybe, knowing more
than it lets on, only playing dead for Block's titillation,
You did it, you conquered, I'm nothing, nothing . . .

until the whirlwind hits and drives them on
obsessed without purpose in their abandon
that could be joy, terror, elation of love, despair's

deflation, desire's movements like armies
maneuvering across no man's land, the spirit
coquetting after the unreachable

as Block now bounds to within an inch of Bag
fluttering off at an eccentric angle,
the light winking off it like an eye winking,

you know I know you know someone's watching—
now Bag crumples in a corner, seemingly blacked out,
Block hovering near as if debating to strike

and demolish Bag, put an end to this pursuit—
no angle of approach, no middle ground,
no terms of ransom, no truce—

just this squarish, brick-faced concrete
among endless displacements rippling out
across this nowhere courtyard where Block and Bag

are at it again, running amok, racing round and round,
giving no quarter and desiring none
the way heroes of old lavish on each other

ferocious attentions no lover can rival,
oh most worthy and wedded of combatants:
berserk Block; shrewd tactician Bag.

Tony Hoagland (1953–2018), "Arrows"

"**LIKE A** sheet of paper, / traveled by blue tongues of flame." The angel/dog tearing at itself "with fast white teeth." The images and phrases here are whatever is the opposite of "ornamental."

Arrows

When a beautiful woman wakes up,
she checks to see if her beauty is still there.
When a sick person wakes up,
he checks to see if he continues to be sick.

He takes the first pills in a thirty-pill day,
looks out the window at a sky
where a time-release sun is crawling
through the milky X ray of a cloud.

•

I sing the body like a burnt-out fuse box,
the wires crossed, the panel lit
by red malfunction lights, the pistons firing
out of sequence,
the warning sirens blatting in the empty halls,

and the hero is trapped in a traffic jam,
the message doesn't reach its destination,
the angel falls down into the body of a dog
and is speechless,

tearing at itself with fast white teeth;
and the consciousness twists evasively,
like a sheet of paper,
      traveled by blue tongues of flame.

•

In the famous painting, the saint
looks steadfastly heavenward,
      away from the physical indignity below,
the fascinating spectacle
  of his own body
        bristling with arrows;

he looks up
as if he were already adamantly elsewhere,
  exerting that power of denial
    the soul is famous for,
that ability to say, "None of this is real:

Nothing that happened here on earth
and who I thought I was,
and nothing that I did or that was done to me,
was ever real."

Atsuro Riley (b. 1960), "Creekthroat"

A MAD mood-music of consonants, and staccato syntax, as in "I lunged I gulped for what I got," telling the story in a spirit of monosyllabic impatience with the conventions of storytelling.

Creekthroat

 —We seen his mama she dry and scant

By hook or by bent
I guttle the rudimental stories.

I'm all in-scoop
suck and swallow by dint of birth. Of shape.

—Were *you* hallow-nursed on riversource
upon a time (or '*the rocky breasts forever*') I was not.

I learned to lie in want
for succor-food; for forms; I lunged I gulped for what I got.

Nowadays to need
to come by what comes by here comes natural and needs no bait.

Just steep dead-still as a blacksnake
creek and wait.

 [*my chokesome weeds, my crook, my lack, my epiphytes, my cypress knees . . .*]

This old appetite as chronic as tides—
on foot or by boat by night (*please*) come slake me with radicle stories.

Natasha Trethewey (b. 1966), *"Kitchen Maid with Supper at Emmaus; or, The Mulata"*

THE PATHOLOGY or delusion of race, embedded in culture and art, becomes a functional reality. The unreal a fountain of realities, the irrational a fountain of reasons.

Kitchen Maid with Supper at Emmaus; or, The Mulata

AFTER THE PAINTING BY DIEGO VELÁZQUEZ, C. 1619

She is the vessels on the table before her:
the copper pot tipped toward us, the white pitcher
clutched in her hand, the black one edged in red
and upside down. Bent over, she is the mortar
and the pestle at rest in the mortar—still angled
in its posture of use. She is the stack of bowls
and the bulb of garlic beside it, the basket hung
by a nail on the wall and the white cloth bundled
in it, the rag in the foreground recalling her hand.
She's the stain on the wall the size of her shadow—
the color of blood, the shape of a thumb. She is echo
of Jesus at table, framed in the scene behind her:
his white corona, her white cap. Listening, she leans
into what she knows. Light falls on half her face.

Major Jackson (b. 1968), "Some Kind of Crazy"

"IT DOESN'T MATTER," given "a community of believers."

Some Kind of Crazy

It doesn't matter if you can't see
Steve's 1985 Corvette: Turquoise-colored,
Plush purple seats, gold-trimmed
Rims that make little stars in your eyes

As if the sun is kneeling, kissing
The edge of sanity. Like a Baptist
Preacher stroking the dark underside
Of God's wet tongue, he can make you

Believe. It's there, his scuffed wing-
Tips—ragged as a mop, shuffling
Concrete—could be ten-inch Firestone
Wheels, his vocal cords fake

An eight-cylinder engine that wags
Like a dog's tail as he shifts gears. Imagine
Steve, moonstruck, cool, turning right
Onto Ridge Avenue, arms forming

Arcs, his hands a set of stiff C's
Overthrowing each other's rule,
His lithe body and head snap back
Pushing a stick shift into fourth

Whizzing past Uncle Sam's Pawn
Shop, past Chung Phat's Stop & Go.
Only he knows his destination,
His limits. Can you see him? Imagine

Steve, moonstruck, cool, parallel,
Parking between a Pacer and a Pinto—
Obviously the most hip—backing up,
Head over right shoulder, one hand

Spinning as if polishing a dream;
And there's Tina, wanting to know
What makes a man tick, wanting
A one-way trip to the stars.

We, the faithful, never call
Him crazy, crackbrained, just a little
Touched. It's all he ever wants:
A car, a girl, a community of believers.

Terrance Hayes (b. 1971), "Mystic Bounce"

WHAT HAPPENS when you bounce from a question instead of answering it? (LM)

Mystic Bounce

Even if you love the racket of ascension,
you must know how the power leaves you.
And at this pitch, who has time for meditation?
The sea walled in by buildings. I do miss
the quiet. Don't you? When I said, "Fuck the deer
antlered and hithered in fur," it was because
I had seen the faces of presidents balled into a fist.
If I were in charge, I would know how to fix
the world: free health care or free physicals,
at least, and an abiding love for the abstract.
When I said, "All of history is saved for us,"
it was because I scorned the emancipated sky.
Does the anthem choke you up? When I asked
God if anyone born to slaves would die
a slave, He said, "Sure as a rock descending
a hillside." That's why I'm not a Christian.

Monica Youn (b. 1971), "Ignatz Invoked"

EVERY SENTENCE, every metaphor here implies that this is a feeling too strong to be merely reasoned with or decorated. Expressive clarity, rather than anecdote, and the furthest thing from mere playing with language.

Ignatz Invoked

A gauze bandage wraps the land
and is unwound, stained orange with sulfates.

A series of slaps molds a mountain,
a fear uncoils itself, testing its long

cool limbs. A passing cloud
seizes up like a carburetor

and falls to earth, lies broken-
backed and lidless in the scree.

Acetylene torches now snug
in their holsters, Shop-Vacs

trundled back behind the dawn.
A mist becomes a murmur, becomes

a moan deepening the dust-
choked fissures in the rock *O pity us*

Ignatz O come to us by moonlight
O arch your speckled body over the earth.

Ange Mlinko (b. 1969), "Dentro de la Tormenta"

LITERALLY, "In the storm." Much gained in translation. The stress-born, barbarous technical term "arbortifacient" has its literal meaning, and its figurative effect.

Dentro de la Tormenta

The revelry of others showed up as
bags under my eyes, flames in glassware
shooting up on this or that terrace
as my own transparent heresy.
The colors were either that of flora
or bath salts; neon was their oracle.
In our room above the café
the bass drops were abortifacient.
One child threw the curtain back,
squealing, "A Lamborghini Huracán!"
and the other, rolling a Matchbox car,
sharing in, then mocking, his ardor,
fabricated a sighting of a Porsche.
Dentro de la tormenta, I saw a woman
braced against wind like an admiral
shouldering ashore, sea foam bullish.
The swimmer was exuberant,
but I wouldn't particularly have wanted
to be that girl having to effect a rescue,
slight, thin-nosed, on lifeguard duty.

Nicole Sealey (b. 1979), "a violence"

THE SEQUENCE "As if," "No," "Yes" at the beginning of sentences is like an underground river of logic, leading to "the mind" and the force of the final lines.

a violence

You hear the high-pitched yowls of strays
fighting for scraps tossed from a kitchen window.
They sound like children you might have had.
Had you wanted children. Had you a maternal bone,
you would wrench it from your belly and fling it
from your fire escape. As if it were the stubborn
shard now lodged in your wrist. No, you would hide it.
Yes, you would hide it inside a barren nesting doll
you've had since you were a child. Its smile
reminds you of your father, who does not smile.
Nor does he believe you are his. "You look just like
your mother," he says, "who looks just like a fire
of suspicious origin." A body, I've read, can sustain
its own sick burning, its own hell, for hours.
It's the mind. It's the mind that cannot.

Patricia Lockwood (b. 1982), "Is Your Country a He or a She in Your Mouth"

THE UNREASON of sexualizing nationalist language, with its monstrous qualities, is mimicked and exposed by the wacky, freestyle reasoning of the poem.

Is Your Country a He or a She in Your Mouth

Mine is a man I think, I love men, they call me
a fatherlandsexual, all the motherlandsexuals
have been sailed away, and there were never
any here in the first place, they tell us. Myself
I have never seen a mountain, myself I have
never seen a valley, especially not my own,
I am afraid of the people who live there,
who eat hawk and wild rice from my pelvic
bone. Oh no, I am fourteen, I have walked
into my motherland's bedroom, her body
is indistinguishable from the fatherland
who is "loving her" from behind, so close
their borders match up, except for a notable
Area belonging to the fatherland. I am drawn
to the motherland's lurid sunsets, I am reaching
my fingers to warm them, the people in my
valley are scooping hawk like crazy, I can no
longer tell which country is which, salt air off
both their coasts, so gross, where is a good nice gulp
of Midwestern pre-tornado? The tornado above me
has sucked up a Cow, the motherland declares,
the tornado above him has sucked up a Bull,
she says pointing to the fatherland. But the cow
is clearly a single cow, chewing a single cud

28

of country, chewing their countries into one,
and "I hate these country!" I scream, and
their eyes shine with rain and fog, because
at last I am using the accent of the homeland,
at last I am a homelandsexual and I will never
go away from them, there will one day be two
of you too they say, but I am boarding myself
already, I recede from their coasts like a Superferry
packed stem to stern with citizens, all waving hellos
and goodbyes, and at night all my people go below
and gorge themselves with hunks of hawk,
the traditional dish of the new floating heartland.

Graham Barnhart (b. 1985), "Pashtu Refresher"

THE RATIONAL shape of a conjugated verb and the rational motive of civil discourse or hospitality: here, like shapes of driftwood afloat in the history-tormented ocean of war, the provisional calm of the armory.

Pashtu Refresher

Zeh dodai khoram

Gatorade bottles like votive candles
half full of toilet paper and dip spit
we chant in the armory classroom

teko dodai khorai

intoning each conjugation with the same
careful automation
used to clean our rifle parts.

hagoi dodai khoree

Bolt scattered to its seven pieces
on a school desk. Gun oil decorates
an altar to the god of preparation.

Zeh dodai khoram
teko dodai khorai
hagoi dodai khoree

I eat food. You eat food.
We eat food like a charm
against ill will in all of its extremes.

GRIEF

Fulke Greville (1554–1628), "Elegy for Philip Sidney"

READ A few lines aloud: the force of poetry, supercharging the meanings of the words in the reader's own breath.

Elegy for Philip Sidney

Silence augmenteth grief, writing increaseth rage,
Staled are my thoughts, which loved and lost the wonder of our age;
Yet quickened now with fire, though dead with frost ere now,
Enraged I write I know not what; dead, quick, I know not how.

Hard-hearted minds relent and rigor's tears abound,
And envy strangely rues his end, in whom no fault was found.
Knowledge her light hath lost, valor hath slain her knight,
Sidney is dead, dead is my friend, dead is the world's delight.

Place, pensive, wails his fall whose presence was her pride;
Time crieth out, My ebb is come; his life was my spring tide.
Fame mourns in that she lost the ground of her reports;
Each living wight laments his lack, and all in sundry sorts.

He was (woe worth that word!) to each well-thinking mind
A spotless friend, a matchless man, whose virtue ever shined;
Declaring in his thoughts, his life, and that he writ,
Highest conceits, longest foresights, and deepest works of wit.

He, only like himself, was second unto none,
Whose death (though life) we rue, and wrong, and all in vain do
    moan;
Their loss, not him, wail they that fill the world with cries,
Death slew not him, but he made death his ladder to the skies.

Now sink of sorrow I who live—the more the wrong!
Who wishing death, whom death denies, whose thread is all too
    long;
Who tied to wretched life, who looks for no relief,
Must spend my ever dying days in never ending grief.

Farewell to you, my hopes, my wonted waking dreams,
Farewell, sometimes enjoyëd joy, eclipsëd are thy beams.
Farewell, self-pleasing thoughts which quietness brings forth,
And farewell, friendship's sacred league, uniting minds of worth.

And farewell, merry heart, the gift of guiltless minds,
And all sports which for life's restore variety assigns;
Let all that sweet is, void; in me no mirth may dwell:
Philip, the cause of all this woe, my life's content, farewell!

Now rhyme, the son of rage, which art no kin to skill,
And endless grief, which deads my life, yet knows not how to kill,
Go, seek that hapless tomb, which if ye hap to find
Salute the stones that keep the limbs that held so good a mind.

Ben Jonson (1572–1637), "On My First Son"

TREMBLING, YET calm: exactly between the impossible extremes of total bereavement and Christian consolation.

On My First Son

Farewell, thou child of my right hand, and joy;
My sin was too much hope of thee, loved boy:
Seven years thou'wert lent to me, and I thee pay,
Exacted by thy fate, on the just day.
O could I lose all father now! for why
Will man lament the state he should envy,
To have so soon 'scaped world's and flesh's rage,
And, if no other misery, yet age?
Rest in soft peace, and asked, say, "Here doth lie
Ben Jonson his best piece of poetry."
For whose sake henceforth all his vows be such
As what he loves may never like too much.

Samuel Johnson (1709–1784), "On the Death of Dr. Robert Levet"

THE QUIET, profound truth of language like "our social comforts."

On the Death of Dr. Robert Levet

Condemned to Hope's delusive mine,
   As on we toil from day to day,
By sudden blasts, or slow decline,
   Our social comforts drop away.

Well tried through many a varying year,
   See Levet to the grave descend;
Officious, innocent, sincere,
   Of every friendless name the friend.

Yet still he fills Affection's eye,
   Obscurely wise, and coarsely kind;
Nor, lettered Arrogance, deny
   Thy praise to merit unrefined.

When fainting Nature called for aid,
   And hovering Death prepared the blow,
His vigorous remedy displayed
   The power of art without the show.

In Misery's darkest cavern known,
   His useful care was ever nigh,
Where hopeless Anguish poured his groan,
   And lonely Want retired to die.

No summons mocked by chill delay,
   No petty gain disdained by pride,
The modest wants of every day
   The toil of every day supplied.

His virtues walked their narrow round,
   Nor made a pause, nor left a void;
And sure the Eternal Master found
   The single talent well employed.

The busy day, the peaceful night,
   Unfelt, uncounted, glided by;
His frame was firm, his powers were bright,
   Though now his eightieth year was nigh.

Then with no throbbing fiery pain,
   No cold gradations of decay,
Death broke at once the vital chain,
   And freed his soul the nearest way.

William Cowper (1731–1800), "Epitaph on a Hare"

HE SINCERELY grieves the loss of Old Tiney, and he also acknowledges the absurd element in that grief—with the contradiction redoubling the pain.

Epitaph on a Hare

Here lies, whom hound did ne'er pursue,
    Nor swifter greyhound follow,
Whose foot ne'er tainted morning dew,
    Nor ear heard huntsman's hallo',

Old Tiney, surliest of his kind,
    Who, nursed with tender care,
And to domestic bounds confined,
    Was still a wild jack-hare.

Though duly from my hand he took
    His pittance every night,
He did it with a jealous look,
    And, when he could, would bite.

His diet was of wheaten bread,
    And milk, and oats, and straw,
Thistles, or lettuces instead,
    With sand to scour his maw.

On twigs of hawthorn he regaled,
    On pippins' russet peel;
And, when his juicy salads failed,
    Sliced carrot pleased him well.

A Turkey carpet was his lawn,
   Whereon he loved to bound,
To skip and gambol like a fawn,
   And swing his rump around.

His frisking was at evening hours,
   For then he lost his fear;
But most before approaching showers,
   Or when a storm drew near.

Eight years and five round-rolling moons
   He thus saw steal away,
Dozing out all his idle noons,
   And every night at play.

I kept him for his humor's sake,
   For he would oft beguile
My heart of thoughts that made it ache,
   And force me to a smile.

But now, beneath this walnut-shade
   He finds his long, last home,
And waits in snug concealment laid,
   Till gentler Puss shall come.

He, still more agèd, feels the shocks
   From which no care can save,
And, partner once of Tiney's box,
   Must soon partake his grave.

Walt Whitman (1819–1892), "When Lilacs Last in the Door-yard Bloom'd"

WALT WHITMAN, the death of Abraham Lincoln: rarely, almost uniquely, a great work of art arises from its great occasion.

When Lilacs Last in the Door-yard Bloom'd

I

When lilacs last in the door-yard bloom'd,
And the great star early droop'd in the western sky in the night,
I mourn'd—and yet shall mourn with ever-returning spring.

O ever-returning spring! trinity sure to me you bring;
Lilac blooming perennial, and drooping star in the west,
And thought of him I love.

2

O powerful, western, fallen star!
O shades of night! O moody, tearful night!
O great star disappear'd! O the black murk that hides the star!
O cruel hands that hold me powerless! O helpless soul of me!
O harsh surrounding cloud, that will not free my soul!

3

In the door-yard fronting an old farm-house, near the white-wash'd
    palings,

Stands the lilac bush, tall-growing, with heart-shaped leaves of rich
    green,
With many a pointed blossom, rising, delicate, with the perfume
    strong I love,
With every leaf a miracle . . . and from this bush in the door-yard,
With delicate-color'd blossoms, and heart-shaped leaves of rich
    green,
A sprig, with its flower, I break.

4

In the swamp, in secluded recesses,
A shy and hidden bird is warbling a song.

Solitary, the thrush,
The hermit, withdrawn to himself, avoiding the settlements,
Sings by himself a song.

Song of the bleeding throat!
Death's outlet song of life—(for well, dear brother, I know
If thou wast not gifted to sing, thou would'st surely die.)

5

Over the breast of the spring, the land, amid cities,
Amid lanes, and through old woods, (where lately the violets
    peep'd from the ground, spotting the gray debris;)
Amid the grass in the fields each side of the lanes—passing the
    endless grass;
Passing the yellow-spear'd wheat, every grain from its shroud in
    the dark-brown fields uprising;
Passing the apple-tree blows of white and pink in the orchards;
Carrying a corpse to where it shall rest in the grave,
Night and day journeys a coffin.

6

Coffin that passes through lanes and streets,
Through day and night, with the great cloud darkening the land,
With the pomp of the inloop'd flags, with the cities draped in black,
With the show of the States themselves, as of crape-veil'd women,
   standing,
With processions long and winding, and the flambeaus of the night,
With the countless torches lit—with the silent sea of faces, and the
   unbared heads,
With the waiting depot, the arriving coffin, and the sombre faces,
With dirges through the night, with the thousand voices rising
   strong and solemn;
With all the mournful voices of the dirges, pour'd around the coffin,
The dim-lit churches and the shuddering organs—Where amid
   these you journey,
With the tolling, tolling bells' perpetual clang;
Here! coffin that slowly passes,
I give you my sprig of lilac.

7

(Nor for you, for one, alone;
Blossoms and branches green to coffins all I bring:
For fresh as the morning—thus would I carol a song for you, O
   sane and sacred death.

All over bouquets of roses,
O death! I cover you over with roses and early lilies;
But mostly and now the lilac that blooms the first,
Copious, I break, I break the sprigs from the bushes;
With loaded arms I come, pouring for you,
For you, and the coffins all of you, O death.)

8

O western orb, sailing the heaven!
Now I know what you must have meant, as a month since we
    walk'd,
As we walk'd up and down in the dark blue so mystic,
As we walk'd in silence the transparent shadowy night,
As I saw you had something to tell, as you bent to me night after
    night,
As you droop'd from the sky low down, as if to my side, (while the
    other stars all look'd on;)
As we wander'd together the solemn night, (for something, I know
    not what, kept me from sleep;)
As the night advanced, and I saw on the rim of the west, ere you
    went, how full you were of woe;
As I stood on the rising ground in the breeze, in the cold
    transparent night,
As I watch'd where you pass'd and was lost in the netherward
    black of the night,
As my soul, in its trouble, dissatisfied, sank, as where you, sad orb,
Concluded, dropt in the night, and was gone.

9

Sing on, there in the swamp!
O singer bashful and tender! I hear your notes—I hear your call;
I hear—I come presently—I understand you;
But a moment I linger—for the lustrous star has detain'd me;
The star, my departing comrade, holds and detains me.

10

O how shall I warble myself for the dead one there I loved?
And how shall I deck my song for the large sweet soul that has gone?
And what shall my perfume be, for the grave of him I love?

Sea-winds, blown from east and west,
Blown from the eastern sea, and blown from the western sea, till
    there on the prairies meeting:
These, and with these, and the breath of my chant,
I perfume the grave of him I love.

11

O what shall I hang on the chamber walls?
And what shall the pictures be that I hang on the walls,
To adorn the burial-house of him I love?
Pictures of growing spring, and farms, and homes,
With the Fourth-month eve at sundown, and the gray smoke lucid
    and bright,
With floods of the yellow gold of the gorgeous, indolent, sinking
    sun, burning, expanding the air;
With the fresh sweet herbage under foot, and the pale green leaves
    of the trees prolific;
In the distance the flowing glaze, the breast of the river, with a
    wind-dapple here and there;
With ranging hills on the banks, with many a line against the sky,
    and shadows;
And the city at hand, with dwellings so dense, and stacks of
    chimneys,
And all the scenes of life, and the workshops, and the workmen
    homeward returning.

12

Lo! body and soul! this land!
Mighty Manhattan, with spires, and the sparkling and hurrying
  tides, and the ships;
The varied and ample land—the South and the North in the
  light—Ohio's shores, and flashing Missouri,
And ever the far-spreading prairies, cover'd with grass and corn.

Lo! the most excellent sun, so calm and haughty;
The violet and purple morn, with just-felt breezes;
The gentle, soft-born, measureless light;
The miracle, spreading, bathing all—the fulfill'd noon;
The coming eve, delicious—the welcome night, and the stars,
Over my cities shining all, enveloping man and land.

13

Sing on! sing on, you gray-brown bird!
Sing from the swamps, the recesses—pour your chant from the
  bushes;
Limitless out of the dusk, out of the cedars and pines.

Sing on, dearest brother—warble your reedy song;
Loud human song, with voice of uttermost woe.

O liquid, and free, and tender!
O wild and loose to my soul! O wondrous singer!
You only I hear . . . yet the star holds me, (but will soon depart;)
Yet the lilac, with mastering odor, holds me.

14

Now while I sat in the day, and look'd forth,
In the close of the day, with its light, and the fields of spring, and
the farmer preparing his crops,
In the large unconscious scenery of my land, with its lakes and
forests,
In the heavenly aerial beauty, (after the perturb'd winds, and the
storms;)
Under the arching heavens of the afternoon swift passing, and the
voices of children and women,
The many-moving sea-tides,—and I saw the ships how they sail'd,
And the summer approaching with richness, and the fields all busy
with labor,
And the infinite separate houses, how they all went on, each with
its meals and minutia of daily usages;
And the streets, how their throbbings throbb'd, and the cities
pent—lo! then and there,
Falling upon them all, and among them all, enveloping me with
the rest,
Appear'd the cloud, appear'd the long black trail;
And I knew Death, its thought, and the sacred knowledge of death.

15

Then with the knowledge of death as walking one side of me,
And the thought of death close-walking the other side of me,
And I in the middle, as with companions, and as holding the hands
of companions,
I fled forth to the hiding receiving night, that talks not,
Down to the shores of the water, the path by the swamp in the
dimness,
To the solemn shadowy cedars, and ghostly pines so still.

And the singer so shy to the rest receiv'd me;
The gray-brown bird I know, receiv'd us comrades three;
And he sang what seem'd the carol of death, and a verse for him I
    love.

From deep secluded recesses,
From the fragrant cedars, and the ghostly pines so still,
Came the carol of the bird.

And the charm of the carol rapt me,
As I held, as if by their hands, my comrades in the night;
And the voice of my spirit tallied the song of the bird.

16

DEATH CAROL.

Come, lovely and soothing Death,
Undulate round the world, serenely arriving, arriving,
In the day, in the night, to all, to each,
Sooner or later, delicate Death.

Prais'd be the fathomless universe,
For life and joy, and for objects and knowledge curious;
And for love, sweet love—But praise! praise! praise!
For the sure-enwinding arms of cool-enfolding Death.

Dark Mother, always gliding near, with soft feet,
Have none chanted for thee a chant of fullest welcome?

Then I chant it for thee—I glorify thee above all;
I bring thee a song that when thou must indeed come, come unfalteringly.

Approach, strong Deliveress!
When it is so—when thou hast taken them, I joyously sing the dead,
Lost in the loving, floating ocean of thee,
Laved in the flood of thy bliss, O Death.

From me to thee glad serenades,
Dances for thee I propose, saluting thee—adornments and feastings for thee;
And the sights of the open landscape, and the high-spread sky, are fitting,
And life and the fields, and the huge and thoughtful night.

The night, in silence, under many a star;
The ocean shore, and the husky whispering wave, whose voice I know;
And the soul turning to thee, O vast and well-veil'd Death,
And the body gratefully nestling close to thee.

Over the tree-tops I float thee a song!
Over the rising and sinking waves—over the myriad fields, and the
    prairies wide;
Over the dense-pack'd cities all, and the teeming wharves and ways,
I float this carol with joy, with joy to thee, O Death!

17

To the tally of my soul,
Loud and strong kept up the gray-brown bird,
With pure, deliberate notes, spreading, filling the night.

Loud in the pines and cedars dim,
Clear in the freshness moist, and the swamp-perfume;
And I with my comrades there in the night.

While my sight that was bound in my eyes unclosed,
As to long panoramas of visions.

18

I saw askant the armies;
And I saw, as in noiseless dreams, hundreds of battle-flags;
Borne through the smoke of the battles, and pierc'd with missiles,
    I saw them,
And carried hither and yon through the smoke, and torn and
    bloody;
And at last but a few shreds left on the staffs, (and all in silence,)
And the staffs all splinter'd and broken.

I saw battle-corpses, myriads of them,
And the white skeletons of young men—I saw them;
I saw the debris and debris of all the dead soldiers of the war;
But I saw they were not as was thought;
They themselves were fully at rest—they suffer'd not;
The living remain'd and suffer'd—the mother suffer'd,
And the wife and the child, and the musing comrade suffer'd,
And the armies that remain'd suffer'd.

19

Passing the visions, passing the night;
Passing, unloosing the hold of my comrades' hands;
Passing the song of the hermit bird, and the tallying song of my
    soul,
(Victorious song, death's outlet song, yet varying, ever-altering
    song,
As low and wailing, yet clear the notes, rising and falling, flooding
    the night,
Sadly sinking and fainting, as warning and warning, and yet again
    bursting with joy,
Covering the earth, and filling the spread of the heaven,
As that powerful psalm in the night I heard from recesses,)

Passing, I leave thee, lilac with heart-shaped leaves;
I leave thee there in the door-yard, blooming, returning with spring,
I cease from my song for thee;
From my gaze on thee in the west, fronting the west, communing
    with thee,
O comrade lustrous, with silver face in the night.

    20

Yet each I keep, and all, retrievements out of the night;
The song, the wondrous chant of the gray-brown bird,
And the tallying chant, the echo arous'd in my soul,
With the lustrous and drooping star, with the countenance full of
    woe,
With the lilac tall, and its blossoms of mastering odor;
With the holders holding my hand, nearing the call of the bird,
Comrades mine, and I in the midst, and their memory ever I
    keep—for the dead I loved so well;
For the sweetest, wisest soul of all my days and lands . . . and this
    for his dear sake;
Lilac and star and bird, twined with the chant of my soul,
There in the fragrant pines, and the cedars dusk and dim.

Emily Dickinson (1830–1886), "It Was Not Death, for I Stood Up" (no. 355)

SOMETIMES A pronoun becomes a great mystery: "it."

355

It was not Death, for I stood up,
And all the Dead, lie down—
It was not Night, for all the Bells
Put out their Tongues, for Noon.

It was not Frost, for on my Flesh
I felt Siroccos—crawl—
Nor Fire—for just my marble feet
Could keep a Chancel, cool—

And yet, it tasted, like them all,
The Figures I have seen
Set orderly, for Burial,
Reminded me, of mine—

As if my life were shaven,
And fitted to a frame,
And could not breathe without a key,
And 'twas like Midnight, some—

When everything that ticked—has stopped
And space stares—all around—
Or Grisly frosts—first Autumn morns,
Repeal the Beating Ground—

But, most, like Chaos—Stopless—cool—
Without a Chance, or spar—
Or even a Report of Land—
To justify—Despair.

Wallace Stevens (1879–1955), "The Emperor of Ice-Cream"

A NOTE of self-parody heightening the chords of grief, the mere flavors of beautiful verses, attributed to the same emperor.

The Emperor of Ice-Cream

Call the roller of big cigars,
The muscular one, and bid him whip
In kitchen cups concupiscent curds.
Let the wenches dawdle in such dress
As they are used to wear, and let the boys
Bring flowers in last month's newspapers.
Let be be finale of seem.
The only emperor is the emperor of ice-cream.

Take from the dresser of deal,
Lacking the three glass knobs, that sheet
On which she embroidered fantails once
And spread it so as to cover her face.
If her horny feet protrude, they come
To show how cold she is, and dumb.
Let the lamp affix its beam.
The only emperor is the emperor of ice-cream.

Edwin Muir (1887–1959), "The Brothers"

THE PLAINNESS of the language and the elaboration of the form: between them, the intense arc of emotion.

The Brothers

Last night I watched my brothers play,
The gentle and the reckless one,
In a field two yards away.
For half a century they were gone
Beyond the other side of care
To be among the peaceful dead.
Even in a dream how could I dare
Interrogate that happiness
So wildly spent yet never less?
For still they raced about the green
And were like two revolving suns;
A brightness poured from head to head,
So strong I could not see their eyes
Or look into their paradise.
What were they doing, the happy ones?
Yet where I was they once had been.

I thought, How could I be so dull,
Twenty thousand days ago,
Not to see they were beautiful?
I asked them, Were you really so
As you are now, that other day?
And the dream was soon away.

For then we played for victory
And not to make each other glad.
A darkness covered every head,

Frowns twisted the original face,
And through that mask we could not see
The beauty and the buried grace.

I have observed in foolish awe
The dateless mid-days of the law
And seen indifferent justice done
By everyone on everyone.
And in a vision I have seen
My brothers playing on the green.

W. H. Auden (1907–1973), "Funeral Blues"

SO THOROUGHLY total that there's some temptation to include the poem under the heading "Manic Laughter"—which is not to deny the intensity of feeling.

Funeral Blues

Stop all the clocks, cut off the telephone,
Prevent the dog from barking with a juicy bone,
Silence the pianos and with muffled drum
Bring out the coffin, let the mourners come.

Let aeroplanes circle moaning overhead
Scribbling on the sky the message He Is Dead,
Put crêpe bows round the white necks of the public doves,
Let the traffic policemen wear black cotton gloves.

He was my North, my South, my East and West,
My working week and my Sunday rest,
My noon, my midnight, my talk, my song;
I thought that love would last for ever: I was wrong.

The stars are not wanted now; put out every one,
Pack up the moon and dismantle the sun,
Pour away the ocean and sweep up the wood;
For nothing now can ever come to any good.

Gwendolyn Brooks (1917–2000), "The Bean Eaters"

WITH THE word "plain" twice in one line, with the rhymes that cleave to the rhythms of speech, the homely details become a great memorial oration.

The Bean Eaters

They eat beans mostly, this old yellow pair.
Dinner is a casual affair.
Plain chipware on a plain and creaking wood,
Tin flatware.

Two who are Mostly Good.
Two who have lived their day,
But keep on putting on their clothes
And putting things away.

And remembering . . .
Remembering, with twinklings and twinges,
As they lean over the beans in their rented back room that
          is full of beads and receipts and dolls and cloths,
          tobacco crumbs, vases and fringes.

Alan Dugan (1923–2003),
"Funeral Oration for a Mouse"

THE LAMENT as a form, lampooned yet fulfilled.

Funeral Oration for a Mouse

This, Lord, was an anxious brother and
a living diagram of fear: full of health himself,
    he brought diseases like a gift
to give his hosts. Masked in a cat's moustache
but sounding like a bird, he was a ghost
    of lesser noises and a kitchen pest
for whom some ladies stand on chairs. So,
Lord, accept our felt though minor guilt
    for an ignoble foe and ancient sin:
    the murder of a guest
who shared our board: just once he ate
    too slowly, dying in our trap
from necessary hunger and a broken back.

Humors of love aside, the mousetrap was our own
opinion of the mouse, but for the mouse
    it was the tree of knowledge with
its consequential fruit, the true cross
and the gate of hell. Even to approach
    it makes him like or better than
its maker: his courage as a spoiler never once
impressed us, but to go out cautiously at night,
    into the dining room—what bravery, what
    hunger! Younger by far, in dying he
was older than us all: his mobile tail and nose
    spasmed in the pinch of our annoyance. Why,

then, at that snapping sound, did we, victorious,
begin to laugh without delight?

Our stomachs, deep in an analysis
of their own stolen baits
(and asking, "Lord, Host, to whom are we the pests?"),
contracted and demanded a retreat
from our machine and its effect of death,
as if the mouse's fingers, skinnier
than hairpins and as breakable as cheese,
could grasp our grasping lives, and in
their drowning movement pull us under too,
into the common death beyond the mousetrap.

Gail Mazur (b. 1937), "Forbidden City"

THE INTENSITY HERE, the feeling of encountering a harsh limit, arises from the starkness of grief, a simplicity that takes command of the dreamlike, the figurative, the allusive.

Forbidden City

Asleep until noon, I'm dreaming
we've been granted another year.

You're here with me, healthy.
Then, half-awake, the half-truth—

this is our last day. Life's leaking
away again, and this time, we know it.

Dear body, I hold you, pleading,
Don't leave! but I understand you

can't say anything. Who are we?
Are we fictional? We don't look

like our pictures, don't look like
anyone I know. Daylight

flickers through a bamboo grove,
we approach the Forbidden City,

looking together for the Hall
of Fulfilling Original Wishes.

Time is the treasure, you tell me,
and the past is its hiding place.

I instruct our fictional children,
The past is the treasure, time

is its hiding place. If we told him
how much we love him, how much

we miss him, he could stay.
But now you've taken me back

to Luoyang, to the Garden of Solitary Joy,
over a thousand years old—

I wake, I hold your hand, you let me go.

Louise Glück (b. 1943), "Visitors from Abroad"

TIME, LIKE the snow in this poem, can magnify griefs rather than obscure them. And haunting can be a manifestation of grief.

Visitors from Abroad

I.

Sometime after I had entered
that time of life
people prefer to allude to in others
but not in themselves, in the middle of the night
the phone rang. It rang and rang
as though the world needed me,
though really it was the reverse.

I lay in bed, trying to analyze
the ring. It had
my mother's persistence and my father's
pained embarrassment.

When I picked it up, the line was dead.
Or was the phone working and the caller dead?
Or was it not the phone, but the door perhaps?

2.

My mother and father stood in the cold
on the front steps. My mother stared at me,
a daughter, a fellow female.
You never think of us, she said.

We read your books when they reach heaven.
Hardly a mention of us anymore, hardly a mention of your sister.
And they pointed to my dead sister, a complete stranger,
tightly wrapped in my mother's arms.

But for us, she said, you wouldn't exist.
And your sister—you have your sister's soul.
After which they vanished, like Mormon missionaries.

3.

The street was white again,
all the bushes covered with heavy snow
and the trees glittering, encased with ice.

I lay in the dark, waiting for the night to end.
It seemed the longest night I had ever known,
longer than the night I was born.

I write about you all the time, I said aloud.
Every time I say "I," it refers to you.

4.

Outside the street was silent.
The receiver lay on its side among the tangled sheets,
its peevish throbbing had ceased some hours before.

I left it as it was;
its long cord drifting under the furniture.

I watched the snow falling,
not so much obscuring things
as making them seem larger than they were.

Who would call in the middle of the night?
Trouble calls, despair calls.
Joy is sleeping like a baby.

Carol Muske-Dukes (b. 1945), "The Illusion"

AS IN Mazur's poem (p. 62), the figurative material—the lost beloved was a professional actor—supplies a contrasting background for the stark reality of loss.

The Illusion

After his death, I kept an illusion before me:
that I would find the key to him, the answer,
in the words of a play that he'd put to heart
years earlier. I'd find the secret place in him,

retracing lines he'd learned, tracking
his prints in snow. I'd discover, scrawled
in the margin of a script, a stage-note that
would clarify consciousness in a single gesture—

not only the playwright's imagery—but his,
the actor's, and his, the self's. Past thought's
proscenium: the slight tilt of Alceste's head or
his too-quick ironic bow; the long pause as Henry

Carr adjusts his straw boater; Salieri slumps at
the keyboard; Hotspur sinks into self-reflection—
where the actor disappears into physical inspiration.
Thought rises, a silent aria; thought glitters in the infinite

prism of representation. For love unrequited and tactical
hate, the shouted curse of a wretched son, a vengeful duke,
in that silent prescient dialogue—unspoken—he'd
show up in the ear, in a tone blue and sweetened as wood-

smoke, show up in these directions to the flesh: cues
like green shouts, the blood swimming with indicatives.
Look—the same smile he flashed at me
from the shaving mirror is here, right here—

but *realized*: I remember this path opening
in a deep forest outside Athens, the moon
shuddering into place—and no players as yet at hand.

Marie Howe (b. 1950), "What the Living Do"

THE SECOND person of elegy made actual: the actual, grieved-for "you."

What the Living Do

Johnny, the kitchen sink has been clogged for days, some utensil
   probably fell down there.
And the Drano won't work but smells dangerous, and the crusty
   dishes have piled up

waiting for the plumber I still haven't called. This is the everyday
   we spoke of.
It's winter again: the sky's a deep headstrong blue, and the sunlight
   pours through

the open living room windows because the heat's on too high in
   here, and I can't turn it off.
For weeks now, driving, or dropping a bag of groceries in the
   street, the bag breaking,

I've been thinking: This is what the living do. And yesterday,
   hurrying along those
wobbly bricks in the Cambridge sidewalk, spilling my coffee down
   my wrist and sleeve,

I thought it again, and again later, when buying a hairbrush: This
   is it.
Parking. Slamming the car door shut in the cold. What you called
   that yearning.

What you finally gave up. We want the spring to come and the
    winter to pass. We want
whoever to call or not call, a letter, a kiss—we want more and
    more and then more of it.

But there are moments, walking, when I catch a glimpse of myself
    in the window glass,
say, the window of the corner video store, and I'm gripped by a
    cherishing so deep

for my own blowing hair, chapped face, and unbuttoned coat that
    I'm speechless:
I am living, I remember you.

Peter Balakian (b. 1951), "Going to Zero"

GRIEF IS not just personal; sometimes it is historical or communal, even civic. This poem is all of the above. Peter Balakian worked as a mailroom assistant in the Twin Towers, years before 9/11.

Going to Zero

I.

A canvas with less turpentine, more hard edges, less bleeding,
that was good for beauty, Frankenthaler in *Art News*

in the dining car crammed with parkas and laptops
microwaved cellophane, plastic plates and canvas bags,

and the valley under fog as the cows disappeared
and when the green came back into view I could see

the SUVs floating on the Thruway, the cows oblivious
to the revved engines of trucks. The river glistened

all the way to Albany, and I could see flags on Baptist churches
and resurrection trailers, "God Bless America" on pickups—

"United We Stand" laminated to billboards
as the fog settled then lifted, and when I woke

a flag the size of a football field hung from the gray tower of the GW,
where the tractor-trailers jammed beneath its hem

as something sifted down on the silver-plated Hudson.
And then the lights went out.

2.

The faces on 7th Avenue blurred in the chaos of vendors and liberty
scarves, freedom ties, glowing plastic torches, dollars and
   polyester—

and inside Macy's I was hit by cool air as "Stars and Stripes Forever"
floated down from women's fashions into the quiet aisles of
   Aramis and silk scarves.

I wanted to buy the Frankenthaler, a modest, early print,
minimal, monochromatic; surface and perspective in dialogue;
on 24th off 10th—the gallery still smelled like wood and plaster—

but I didn't stop, and when the train reached the Stock Exchange
the Yom Kippur streets were quiet, and the bronze statue of
   Washington
was camouflaged by national guard. I was walking my old mail
   route now

like a drunk knocking into people, almost hit by a cab
until the roped-off streets cut me at the arm. At Broadway and
   Liberty
the fences wound around the bursts of dust rising

over the cranes and bulldozers, over the punched-out windows—
I stared through a piece of rusted grid that stood like a gate to the
   crystal river.
I was sweating in my sweatshirt now, the hood filling with soot,

as I watched with others drinking Cokes and eating their pizza of
   disbelief.
Zero began with the Sumerians who made circles with hollow reeds
in wet clay and baked them for posterity.

At Broadway and Liberty. At 20 floors charred and standing.
At miasma people weeping. Anna's Nail Salon, Daikichi Sushi,
the vacant shops, stripped clean in the graffiti of dust-coated
    windows.

Something blasted from a boom box in a music store,
something, in the ineffable clips of light,
disappeared over the river.

Robert Wrigley (b. 1951), "Cemetery Moles"

THE TITLE'S unsettling, maybe outrageous suggestion builds to ful-
fillment in the outrageous image of the conclusion. The grief is in a
way generalized and in a way particular, though unspecified.

Cemetery Moles

Most are not blind, but still,
might the concrete burial vaults
be perceived before a tunnel
comes to such a sudden hard naught?

Though I notice their mounds mostly
down here with the old stones, last row—
those graves that are not only
vaultless but with a wooden casket too.

And the stories from the sexton?
A filled tooth on a hill whitely shining,
and a mole in a trap one early June,
around its neck a wedding ring.

Marilyn Chin (b. 1955),
from "Beautiful Boyfriend"

WALKING AN elusive line between profusion and oblivion. (LM)

from "Beautiful Boyfriend"

FOR DON LONE WOLF (1958–2011)

My skiff is made of spicewood   my oars are Cassia bract
Music flows   from bow to starboard
Early Mozart   cool side of Coltrane   and miles and miles
   of Miles
Cheap Californian Merlot   and my new boyfriend

•

If I could master   the nine doors of my body
And close my heart   to the cries of suffering
Perhaps   I could love you like no other
Float my mind   toward the other side of hate

•

The shanty towns of Tijuana   sing for you
The slums of Little Sudan   hold evening prayer
One dead brown boy is a tragedy
   Ten thousand is a statistic
So let's fuck   my love   until the dogs pass

•

All beautiful boyfriends are transitory
They have no souls   they're shiny brown flesh
Tomorrow they'll turn into   purple festering corpses
Fissured   gored   by a myriad flies

•

Down the Irrawaddy River   you lay yourself to sleep
No sun no moon   no coming no going
No causality   no personality
No hunger   no thirst

•

Malarial deltas   typhoidal cays
Tsunamis don't judge   Calamity grieves no one
The poor will be submerged   the rich won't be saved
Purge the innocent   sink the depraved

•

What do I smell   but the perfume of transience
Crushed calyxes   rotting phloems
Let's write   pretty poems   pretty poems   pretty poems
Masque stale pogroms   with a sweet whiff of oblivion

James Longenbach (b. 1959), "Lyric Knowledge"

THE ORDER brought by removals, the order enforced by time, the order of memory, the order of exchange: all defy any one person's will. Knowledge as choral, not enumerative or linear.

Lyric Knowledge

Finally having cleaned out the closet, I awoke
To find it filled with things.
Somebody else might need those things,
So I put them in a box, I put the box at the curb.

The following morning, after breakfast, the closet once again was full.
Once again I cleaned it, this time retaining things
Unfamiliar to me, discarding the rest.

In my mind, these acts of accumulation transpired
As quickly as the acts of dispersal,
A single night, a single day.
In fact they took many years.

In one of those years I wrote a book.
Rather than discarding things
Outright, I redeployed them, altering their function.

But at the end of the year I nonetheless found myself at the curb.
I greeted my neighbors, I was greeted in turn.

Together we watched the cars go by.
The cars followed the road. Above our heads
The leaves turned silver in the breeze.

Nick Flynn (b. 1960), "Sudden"

THE LAST two lines give a striking feeling of an absolute end: the abrupt ampersands and the clashing images of ringing and eating, finality and clamor.

Sudden

If it had been a heart attack, the newspaper
might have used the word *massive,*
      as if a mountain range had opened
          inside her, but instead

it used the word *suddenly,* a light coming on

in an empty room. The telephone

fell from my shoulder, a black parrot repeating
         something happened, something awful

    a sunday, dusky. If it had been

terminal, we could have cradled her
as she grew smaller, wiped her mouth,

      said good-bye. But it was *sudden,*

how overnight we could be orphaned
& the world become a bell we'd crawl inside
& the ringing all we'd eat.

Joshua Weiner (b. 1963),
"Postcard to Thom"

GRIEF FINDING its way into laughter and into the weird, expressive
sexual fantasia of an ancient image on the unsent postcard.

Postcard to Thom

Addressed, it lately sits propped on my desk
with no reason now to go—you're gone, somewhere
behind the snow screen, though I think you'd laugh
at this lucky charm from Herculaneum
suspended by a chain in opened doors
even the bravest might have fled through—
a gladiator, and in both raised fists
a knife to strike himself, his own huge leaping
cock curving up with a snarling panther's head
to savage the source of its awakening:
the mind, alarm of want ringing the blood
as appetite grows to feel itself grow longer,
twisting back on the hot stone of the heart.
And dangling down from panther cock, each foot,
the muscled back and swollen scrotal sac—
a little bell provoked by the cooling wind.

Jenny George (b. 1978), "One-Way Gate"

THE NARRATIVE is quiet. The contrast between that and the meaning of the final phrases is immense.

One-Way Gate

I was moving the herd from the lower pasture
to the loading pen up by the road.
It was cold and their mouths steamed like torn bread.
The gate swung on its wheel, knocking at the herd
as they pushed through. They stomped
and pocked the freezing mud with their hooves.
This was January. I faced backward into the hard year.
The herd faced forward as the herd always does,
muscling through the lit pane of winter air.

It could have been any gate, any moment when things go
one way and not the other—an act of tenderness
or a small, cruel thing done with a pocketknife.
A child being born. Or the way we move
from sleeping to dreams, as a river flows uneasy under ice.

Of course, nothing can ever be returned to exactly.
In the pen the herd nosed the fence and I forked them hay.
A few dry snowflakes swirled the air. The truck would be there
in an hour. Hey, good girl. Go on. Get on, girl.

LOVE
AND
RAGE

Sappho (c. 630–c. 570 BC), "Artfully Adorned Aphrodite," translated by Jim Powell

"**WHAT IS** it this time," says the overworked deity of love. Aphrodite is a projection or cloak of the lover's rage, transformed into the amused impatience of the goddess.

Artfully Adorned Aphrodite

Artfully adorned Aphrodite, deathless
child of Zeus and weaver of wiles I beg you
please don't hurt me, don't overcome my spirit,
     goddess, with longing,

but come here, if ever at other moments
hearing these my words from afar you listened
and responded: leaving your father's house, all
     golden, you came then,

hitching up your chariot: lovely sparrows
drew you quickly over the dark earth, whirling
on fine beating wings from the heights of heaven
     down through the sky and

instantly arrived—and then O my blessed
goddess with a smile on your deathless face you
asked me what the matter was *this* time, what I
     called you for this time,

what I now most wanted to happen in my
raving heart: "Whom *this* time should I persuade to

lead you back again to her love? Who *now*, oh
        Sappho, who wrongs you?

If she flees you now, she will soon pursue you;
if she won't accept what you give, she'll give it;
if she doesn't love you, she'll love you soon now,
        even unwilling."

Come to me again, and release me from this
want past bearing. All that my heart desires to
happen—make it happen. And stand beside me,
        goddess, my ally.

Fulke Greville (1554–1628),
Caelica LXIX ("When all this All")

AS IF someone had said, about disappointment in love, "Well, it isn't like it's the end of the world, is it?" . . . and the poet's answer: "Yes it is."

Caelica *LXIX*

When all this All doth pass from age to age,
And revolution in a circle turn,
Then heavenly justice doth appear like rage,
The caves do roar, the very seas do burn,
  Glory grows dark, the sun becomes a night,
  And makes this great world feel a greater might.

When love doth change his seat from heart to heart,
And worth about the Wheel of Fortune goes,
Grace is diseas'd, desert seems overthwart,
Vows are forlorn, and truth doth credit lose,
  Chance then gives law, desire must be wise,
  And look more ways than one, or lose her eyes.

My age of joy is past, of woe begun,
Absence my presence is, strangeness my grace,
With them that walk against me, is my sun:
The wheel is turn'd, I hold the lowest place,
  What can be good to me since my love is,
  To do me harm, content to do amiss?

Michael Drayton (1563–1631), "Three Sorts of Serpents Do Resemble Thee"

IN THE tradition of sonnets, ritual seduction by wit: asking the courted one to feel flattered by, to admire, the artful insults, the dazzling exaggerations.

Three Sorts of Serpents Do Resemble Thee

Three sorts of serpents do resemble thee:
That dangerous eye-killing cockatrice,
The enchanting siren, which doth so entice,
The weeping crocodile—these vile pernicious three.
The basilisk his nature takes from thee,
Who for my life in secret wait dost lie,
And to my heart sendst poison from thine eye:
Thus do I feel the pain, the cause, yet cannot see.
Fair-maid no more, but Mer-maid be thy name,
Who with thy sweet alluring harmony
Hast played the thief, and stolen my heart from me,
And like a tyrant makst my grief thy game:
    Thou crocodile, who when thou hast me slain,
    Lamentst my death, with tears of thy disdain.

Ben Jonson (1572–1637),
"My Picture Left in Scotland"

IN A variation on the ritual of seductively inventive insults—the
flattery that is hyperbolic complaint—the poet's sentences and lines
perform their intricate harmonies to show how deaf the beloved
seems to be.

My Picture Left in Scotland

I now think Love is rather deaf than blind,
    For else it could not be
        That she,
Whom I adore so much, should so slight me
    And cast my love behind.
I'm sure my language to her was as sweet,
    And every close did meet
  In sentence of as subtle feet,
    As hath the youngest He
That sits in shadow of Apollo's tree.

    O, but my conscious fears,
      That fly my thoughts between,
      Tell me that she hath seen
    My hundred of gray hairs,
     Told seven and forty years,
  Read so much waist, as she cannot embrace
    My mountain belly and my rocky face;
And all these through her eyes have stopp'd her ears.

Anne Bradstreet (1612–1672), "Before the Birth of One of Her Children"

REALISTIC, IN THAT time, to anticipate the possible next wife and stepmother. At the notion of that possibility the poet, you might say, quietly rages.

Before the Birth of One of Her Children

All things within this fading world hath end,
Adversity doth still our joys attend;
No ties so strong, no friends so dear and sweet,
But with death's parting blow is sure to meet.
The sentence past is most irrevocable,
A common thing, yet oh inevitable;
How soon, my dear, death may my steps attend,
How soon't may be thy lot to lose thy friend;
We both are ignorant, yet love bids me
These farewell lines to recommend to thee,
That when that knot's untied that made us one,
I may seem thine, who in effect am none.
And if I see not half my days that's due,
What nature would, God grant to yours and you;
The many faults that well you know I have,
Let be interr'd in my oblivion's grave;
If any worth or virtue were in me,
Let that live freshly in thy memory,
And when thou feel'st no grief, as I no harms,
Yet love thy dead, who long lay in thine arms:
And when thy loss shall be repaid with gains,
Look to my little babes, my dear remains.
And if thou love thy self, or loved'st me,

These O protect from step-dame's injury.
And if chance to thine eyes shall bring this verse,
With some sad sighs honor my absent Hearse;
And kiss this paper for thy love's dear sake,
Who with salt tears this last farewell did take.

Aphra Behn (1640–1689), "Love Armed"

THE SONNET TRADITION'S roles of suffering poet and cruel beloved, distilled to its basic duality—without gender pronouns (and in sixteen lines) by a woman poet.

Love Armed

Love in fantastic triumph sat
Whilst bleeding hearts around him flowed,
For whom fresh pains he did create
And strange tyrannic power he showed.

From thy bright eyes he took the fires
Which round about in sport he hurled,
But 'twas from mine he took desires
Enough t'undo the amorous world.

From me he took his sighs and tears,
From thee his pride and cruelty;
From me his languishments and fears.
And every killing dart from thee.

Thus thou and I the God have armed
And set him up a deity;
But my poor heart alone is harmed,
Whilst thine the victor is, and free.

Elizabeth Barrett Browning (1806–1861), "To George Sand"

THE REBELLIOUS French novelist who took a man's name thrills and excites the English poet—who also feels a kind of wistful torment about Sand's sexual and literary daring.

To George Sand

Thou large-brained woman and large-hearted man,
Self-called George Sand! whose soul, amid the lions
Of thy tumultuous senses, moans defiance
And answers roar for roar, as spirits can:
I would some mild miraculous thunder ran
Above the applauded circus, in appliance
Of thine own nobler nature's strength and science,
Drawing two pinions, white as wings of swan,
From thy strong shoulders, to amaze the place
With holier light! that thou to woman's claim
And man's, mightst join beside the angel's grace
Of a pure genius sanctified from blame
Till child and maiden pressed to thine embrace
To kiss upon thy lips a stainless fame.

Emily Dickinson (1830–1886), "I Cannot Live with You" (no. 640)

THE PLAIN and the strange making an extended, unforgettable gesture.

640

I cannot live with You—
It would be Life—
And Life is over there—
Behind the Shelf

The Sexton keeps the key to—
Putting up
Our Life—His Porcelain—
Like a Cup—

Discarded of the Housewife—
Quaint—or Broke—
A newer Sevres pleases—
Old Ones crack—

I could not die—with You—
For One must wait
To shut the Other's Gaze down—
You—could not—

And I—Could I stand by
And see You—freeze—
Without my Right of Frost—
Death's privilege?

Nor could I rise—with You—
Because Your Face
Would put out Jesus'—
That New Grace

Glow plain—and foreign
On my homesick eye—
Except that You than He
Shone closer by—

They'd judge Us—How—
For You—served Heaven—You know,
Or sought to—
I could not—

Because You saturated sight—
And I had no more eyes
For sordid excellence
As Paradise

And were You lost, I would be—
Though my name
Rang loudest
On the Heavenly fame—

And were You—saved—
And I—condemned to be
Where You were not
That self—were Hell to me—

So we must meet apart
You there—I—here—
With just the Door ajar
That Oceans are—and Prayer—
And that White Sustenance—
Despair—

Lionel Johnson (1867–1902), "The Destroyer of a Soul"

RHETORIC OF an extreme—sincere but also *relished*.

The Destroyer of a Soul

I hate you with a necessary hate.
First, I sought patience: passionate was she:
My patience turned in very scorn of me,
That I should dare forgive a sin so great,
As this, through which I sit disconsolate;
Mourning for that live soul, I used to see;
Soul of a saint, whose friend I used to be:
Till you came by! a cold, corrupting, fate.

Why come you now? You, whom I cannot cease
With pure and perfect hate to hate? Go, ring
The death-bell with a deep, triumphant toll!
Say you, my friend sits by me still? Ah, peace!
Call you this thing my friend? this nameless thing?
This living body, hiding its dead soul?

Edna St. Vincent Millay (1892–1950), "I, Being Born a Woman and Distressed"

THE SONNET traditionally involves aggression, if only in the form of seduction: the male poet elaborating the lady's cruel resistance. For example, unlike Michael Drayton (p. 86), Millay, rather than elaborating on the relationship in that old convention, dismisses it. This is a (possibly seductive) rhetoric of indifference, rather than suffering or mock-invective.

I, Being Born a Woman and Distressed

I, being born a woman and distressed
By all the needs and notions of my kind,
Am urged by your propinquity to find
Your person fair, and feel a certain zest
To bear your body's weight upon my breast:
So subtly is the fume of life designed,
To clarify the pulse and cloud the mind,
And leave me once again undone, possessed.
Think not for this, however, the poor treason
Of my stout blood against my staggering brain,
I shall remember you with love, or season
My scorn with pity,—let me make it plain:
I find this frenzy insufficient reason
For conversation when we meet again.

Louise Bogan (1897–1970), "Men Loved Wholly Beyond Wisdom"

"WHOLLY BEYOND" and proud of it.

Men Loved Wholly Beyond Wisdom

Men loved wholly beyond wisdom
Have the staff without the banner.
Like a fire in a dry thicket
Rising within women's eyes
Is the love men must return.
Heart, so subtle now, and trembling,
What a marvel to be wise,
To love never in this manner!
To be quiet in the fern
Like a thing gone dead and still,
Listening to the prisoned cricket
Shake its terrible, dissembling
Music in the granite hill.

Sterling Brown (1901–1989), "Harlem Happiness"

RACIAL EXPECTATIONS and stereotypes, submerged in a romantic idyll for these young lovers, but not forgotten.

Harlem Happiness

I think there is in this the stuff for many lyrics:—
A dago fruit stand at three A.M.; the wop asleep, his woman
Knitting a tiny garment, laughing when we approached her,
Flashing a smile from white teeth, then weighing out the grapes,
Grapes large as plums, and tart and sweet as—well we know the
    lady
And purplish red and firm, quite as this lady's lips are. . . .
We laughed, all three when she awoke her swarthy, snoring Pietro
To make us change, which we, rich paupers, left to help the
    garment.
We swaggered off; while they two stared, and laughed in
    understanding,
And thanked us lovers who brought back an old Etrurian
    springtide.
Then, once beyond their light, a step beyond their pearly smiling
We tasted grapes and tasted lips, and laughed at sleepy Harlem,
And when the huge Mick cop stomped by, a'swingin' of his billy
You nodded to him gaily, and I kissed you with him looking,
Beneath the swinging light that weakly fought against the mist
That settled on Eighth Avenue, and curled around the houses.
And he grinned too and understood the wisdom of our madness.
That night at least the world was ours to spend, nor were we misers.
Ah, Morningside with Maytime awhispering in the foliage!
Alone, atop the city,—the tramps were still in shelter—
And moralizing lights that peered up from the murky distance

Seemed soft as our two cigarette ends burning slowly, dimly,
And careless as the jade stars that winked upon our gladness. . . .

And when I flicked my cigarette, and we watched it falling, falling,
It seemed a shooting meteor, that we, most proud creators
Sent down in gay capriciousness upon a trivial Harlem—

And then I madly quoted lyrics from old kindred masters,
Who wrote of you, unknowing you, for far more lucky me—
And you sang broken bits of song, and we both slept in snatches,
And so the night sped on too swift, with grapes, and words and
    kisses,
And numberless cigarette ends glowing in the darkness
Old Harlem slept regardless, but a motherly old moon—
Shone down benevolently on two happy wastrel lovers. . . .

Robert Hayden (1913–1980), "Those Winter Sundays"

"AUSTERE" AND "OFFICES"—the ardor of cold words. The beautiful formality of "no one," as distinct from the more colloquial "nobody."

Those Winter Sundays

Sundays too my father got up early
and put his clothes on in the blueblack cold,
then with cracked hands that ached
from labor in the weekday weather made
banked fires blaze. No one ever thanked him.

I'd wake and hear the cold splintering, breaking.
When the rooms were warm, he'd call,
and slowly I would rise and dress,
fearing the chronic angers of that house,

Speaking indifferently to him,
who had driven out the cold
and polished my good shoes as well.
What did I know, what did I know
of love's austere and lonely offices?

Alan Dugan (1923–2003), "Love Song: I and Thou"

A MAESTRO of directness at work, with crafty angles and undertones.

Love Song: I and Thou

Nothing is plumb, level, or square:
　　the studs are bowed, the joists
are shaky by nature, no piece fits
　　any other piece without a gap
or pinch, and bent nails
　　dance all over the surfacing
like maggots. By Christ
　　I am no carpenter. I built
the roof for myself, the walls
　　for myself, the floors
for myself, and got
　　hung up in it myself. I
danced with a purple thumb
　　at this house-warming, drunk
with my prime whiskey: rage.
　　Oh I spat rage's nails
into the frame-up of my work:
　　it held. It settled plumb,
level, solid, square and true
　　for that great moment. Then
it screamed and went on through,
　　skewing as wrong the other way.
God damned it. This is hell,
　　but I planned it, I sawed it,
I nailed it, and I
　　will live in it until it kills me.

I can nail my left palm
    to the left-hand crosspiece but
I can't do everything myself.
    I need a hand to nail the right,
a help, a love, a you, a wife.

J. D. McClatchy (1945–2018), "Fado"

THE DANCE of stanzas and rhymes, ardently expressive.

Fado

Suppose my heart had broken
Out of its cage of bone,
Its heaving grille of rumors—
    My metronome,

My honeycomb and crypt
Of jealousies long since
Preyed on, played out,
    My spoiled prince.

Suppose then I could hold it
Out towards you, could feel
Its growling hound of blood
    Brought to heel,

Its scarred skin grown taut
With anticipating your touch,
The tentative caress
    Or sudden clutch.

Suppose you could watch it burn,
A jagged crown of flames
Above the empty rooms
    Where counterclaims

Of air and anger feed
The fire's quickening flush

And into whose remorse
    Excuses rush.

Would you then stretch your hand
To take my scalding gift?
And would you kiss the blackened
    Hypocrite?

It's yours, it's yours—this gift,
This grievance embedded in each,
Where time will never matter
    And words can't reach.

Erin Belieu (b. 1967), "Liar's Karma"

FROM THE first two words, it is clear that this is not a mild, passing attachment or alienation.

Liar's Karma

Assassin, asshole, fine craftsman of myth and malice,
old friend of many years, what was your cause,

Iago? And that afternoon, ear glued to the door, you
spying while he took me hard against the other side,

is that what made you vicious? Did you want him, too?
I'll never know your reasons. But now you live with them,

alone in a peeling bungalow that reeks of the animals who
shit themselves twice daily trying to love you, where a snake

with your mother's face coils like a Freudian cartoon
in the crumbs behind your stove. From the street, I see

you've taken down the curtains in your living room, afraid
of what they're keeping out, but watch how the sunlight bends

around your windows, unwilling to waste itself on dirt
where nothing grows. Consider this your permanent address,

in stunted rooms where fear barely scrapes up the mortgage
and envy ties a hangman's full Windsor around

your neck. Trust me, you'll suffer that silky tongue, friend.
It's the sorrow you made me, the knot frenching your throat.

A. E. Stallings (b. 1968), "First Miracle"

THE INTERTANGLED roots of love and violence, helplessness and want: the poem presents them in a way that can be taken as Christian, or primal, or both.

First Miracle

Her body like a pomegranate torn
Wide open, somehow bears what must be born,

The irony where a stranger small enough
To bed down in the ox-tongue-polished trough

Erupts into the world and breaks the spell
Of the ancient, numbered hours with his yell.

Now her breasts ache and weep and soak her shirt
Whenever she hears his hunger or his hurt;

She can't change water into wine; instead
She fashions sweet milk out of her own blood.

Cate Marvin (b. 1969), "Mug Shot"

THE SONNET FORM updated and savaged a bit, but retaining the traditional turns and the traditional extended metaphor: wounded-love anger and its doings likened to a violent crime, "serious and true."

Mug Shot

Face a distortion. Expression falling back into distance,
as a crowd recedes behind a fleeing man. Iris's brown
black back at the flash, and a hoard of curses perched
on the brink of lip. The mouth cruelly fixed and stained
with an outline of dark lipstick, and in her eyes a light
stirred with the throb of siren's pulse, its mix of glee
and negligence an affront to any decent citizen. A face
crumbling like an old shed begging to be knocked down

with a single kick. Eyes roaming the room as one surveys
land standing neck-deep in a pit, whisky-pitched, ether-lit.
This, as a whole, pulled into the second's suck of lens:
while mirth crawled the halls of countenance, sorrows
flowered behind the brow, and a deadly apathy took up
residence, a serious and true crime was being planned.

The poem on page 107, Kevin Young's "The Hunch," should be formatted as follows:

The Hunch

She wore red like a razor—
cut quite a figure

standing there, her
slender danger

dividing day
from night, there

from here. Where
I hoped to be is near

her & her
fragrant, flammable hair—

words like *always*
entering my mouth

that once only gargled doubt.

You see, I been used
before like a car . . .

Between us
this sweating, a grandfather

clock's steady tick, soundtrack
of saxophones sighing.

It's been too long—
a whole week

since love burned
me like rye. I had begun

to see the glass
as never empty

& that scared me.

She fills me
like the lake

fills a canoe—
no rescue—& to swim

I never learned how.

Kevin Young (b. 1970), "The Hunch"

THE LOVE-COMPLAINT in stoical guise: the idiom of tough-guy detective fiction converted to the emotional material of love sonnets.

The Hunch

She wore red like a razor—cut quite a figure
standing there, her slender danger
dividing day from night, there
from here. Where I hoped to be is near
her & her fragrant, flammable hair—
words like *always* entering my mouth
that once only gargled doubt.
You see, I been used before like a car . . .
Between us, this sweating, a grandfather clock's steady tick,
     soundtrack of saxophones sighing.
It's been too long—a whole week
since love burned me like rye. I had begun
to see the glass as never empty
& that scared me.
She fills me like the lake
fills a canoe—no rescue—& to swim
I never learned how.

Dan Chiasson (b. 1971), "Father and Son"

UNLIKE THE father in Robert Hayden's poem (p. 99), this father was always absent, the two people "nothing" to one another. And when that nothing ends, with death: love and rage in a void.

Father and Son

Only much later did they see, the two of them,
That never knowing one another, there was nothing

Not to know; that not being to begin with meant
Those later, more drastic negations negated nothing;

This was to be the poignant part of it: nothing
Nevertheless would someday end; and the wish—

He wished it in a priory, he wished it in a mall—
Was that when nothing ended it might be

If not an event, at least not a nonevent.
Which, in the end, when it happened, it wasn't.

John Murillo (b. 1971), "Upon Reading That Eric Dolphy Transcribed Even the Calls of Certain Species of Birds,"

THE SURFACE suggests earnest but uncertain talking, with its "I mean," and "Anyway, I'm digressing," and "truth is," and "Let me try this another way." But as with the music of Eric Dolphy, purpose generates purpose, intention becomes a form of discovery, and improvisation is a lofty form of composition.

Upon Reading That Eric Dolphy Transcribed Even the Calls of Certain Species of Birds,

I think first of two sparrows I met when walking home,
late night years ago, in another city, not unlike this—the one

bird frantic, attacking I thought, the way she swooped
down, circled my head, and flailed her wings in my face;

how she seemed to scream each time I swung; how she
dashed back and forth between me and a blood-red Corolla

parked near the opposite curb; how, finally, I understood:
I spied another bird, also calling, its foot inexplicably

caught in the car's closed door, beating its whole bird
body against it. Trying, it appeared, to bang himself free.

And who knows how long he'd been there, wailing. Who
knows—he and the other I mistook, at first, for a bat.

They called to me—something between squawk and chirp,
something between song and prayer—to do something,

anything. And, like any good god, I disappeared. Not
indifferent, exactly. But with things to do. And, most likely,

on my way home from another heartbreak. Call it 1997,
and say I'm several thousand miles from home. By which

I mean those were the days I made of everyone a love song.
By which I mean I was lonely and unrequited. But that's

not quite it either. Truth is, I did manage to find a few
to love me, but couldn't always love them back. The Rasta

law professor. The firefighter's wife. The burlesque dancer
whose daughter blackened drawings with *m*s to mean

the sky was full of birds the day her daddy died. I think
his widow said he drowned one morning on a fishing trip.

Anyway, I'm digressing. But if you asked that night—
did I mention it was night?—why I didn't even try

to jimmy the lock to spring the sparrow, I couldn't say,
truthfully, that it had anything to do with envy, with wanting

a woman to plead as deeply for me as these sparrows did,
one for the other. No. I'd have said something, instead,

about the neighborhood itself, the car thief shot a block
and a half east the week before. Or about the men

I came across nights prior, sweat-slicked and shirtless,
grappling in the middle of the street, the larger one's chest

pressed to the back of the smaller, bruised and bleeding
both. I know you thought this was about birds,

but stay with me. I left them both in the street—
the same street where I'd leave the sparrows—the men

embracing and, for all one knows (especially one not
from around there), they could have been lovers—

the one whispering an old, old tune into the ear
of the other—*Baby, baby, don't leave me this way.* I left

the men where I'd leave the sparrows and their song.
And as I walked away, I heard one of the men call to me,

please or *help* or *brother* or some such. And I didn't break
stride, not one bit. It's how I've learned to save myself.

Let me try this another way. Call it 1977. And say
I'm back west, South Central Los Angeles. My mother

and father at it again. But this time in the street,
broad daylight, and all the neighbors watching. One,

I think his name was Sonny, runs out from his duplex
to pull my father off. You see where I'm going with this?

My mother crying out, fragile as a sparrow. Sonny
fighting my father, fragile as a sparrow. And me,

years later, trying to get it all down. As much for you—
I'm saying—as for me. Sonny catches a left, lies flat

on his back, blood starting to pool and his own
wife wailing. My mother wailing, and traffic backed,

now, half a block. Horns, whistles, and soon sirens.
1977. Summer. And all the trees full of birds. Hundreds,

I swear. And since I'm the one writing it, I'll tell you
they were crying. Which brings me back to Dolphy

and his transcribing. The jazzman, I think, wanted only
to get it down pure. To get it down exact—the animal

racking itself against a car's steel door, the animals
in the trees reporting, the animals we make of ourselves

and one another. Stay with me now. Don't leave me.
Days after the dustup, my parents took me to the park.

And in this park was a pond, and in this pond were birds.
Not sparrows, but swans. And my father spread a blanket

and brought from a basket some apples and a paring knife.
Summertime. My mother wore sunglasses. And long sleeves.

My father, now sober, cursed himself for leaving the radio.
But my mother forgave him, and said, as she caressed

the back of his hand, that we could just listen to the swans.
And we listened. And I watched. Two birds coupling,

one beating its wings as it mounted the other. Summer,
1977. I listened. And watched. When my parents made love

late into that night, I covered my ears in the next room,
scanning the encyclopedia for swans. It meant nothing to me—

then, at least—but did you know the collective noun
for swans is a *lamentation*? And is a lamentation not

its own species of song? What a woman wails, punch drunk
in the street? Or what a widow might sing, learning her man

was drowned by swans? A lamentation of them? Imagine
the capsized boat, the panicked man, struck about the eyes,

nose, and mouth each time he comes up for air. Imagine
the birds coasting away and the waters suddenly calm.

Either trumpet swans or mutes. The dead man's wife
running for help, crying to any who'd listen. A lamentation.

And a city busy saving itself. I'm digressing, sure. But
did you know that to digress means to stray from the flock?

When I left my parents' house, I never looked back. By which
I mean I made like a god and disappeared. As when I left

the sparrows. And the copulating swans. As when someday
I'll leave this city. Its every flailing, its every animal song.

Shane McCrae (b. 1975), "Between"

AT THE different kinds of extreme marked by the words "Nazi" and "love" and "white," the poem chooses something like understatement with the repeated adverb "barely," the judicious tercets, the careful precision of locating the three people in space, even, in a way, the clause "I watched from the sky." The cadences of detachment and intimacy convey the raging, explosive forces that make the very thought of empathy something to dread.

Between

I stood on the bridge in the sky on the bridge between
Two buildings   at the second floor but in
Between the buildings so in neither one

But in the sky   on the second floor in the sky
Barely I had just barely   stepped from the
Nordstrom to cross to the food court barely and I

Now I stood looking down   still   looking down
At the white boy with the Nazi armband on
Below me   to my right below me then

I turned and he was right in front of me
A floor below me   smoking talking we
Would have stood face to face him turned away

From me and to my right away   and smiling
Talking to the white girl leaning   against the wall her
Back against the wall him turning also

Sometimes away from her   and to her right
To blow his smoke away from her his   left
They stood so close together they might have kissed

They didn't kiss   I watched from the sky   but they
Still might have loved   each other I watched afraid
That if they loved each other I would see

Vanesha Pravin (b. 1975), "The Arrangement"

POLYGAMY, IN its culture, with its channels and barriers of love, loyalty, possession, rage, and endurance. In Pravin's poem, the voice of the poet in its elegant English verses incorporates the names of the characters and the meaningful name of the child. Each love and each rage unique, the poem implies, and each with its cultural meaning.

The Arrangement

Late afternoons hiss—the two wives simmer
Raw milk and water, with the dust of tea leaves,

With bruised ginger, cardamom, ground peppercorns,
The cloves floating on top, woody and whole.

Hot chai to be drunk under the tamarind, the pods
Phallic, dangling, their pulp used for chutney.

In the evening, the air cool for a walk, Kunku
Leaves Jiba alone with Harilal, whose children

Are born to two mothers. The youngest, a girl—
Her name *Santha* means *calm, pacified.*

Wendy Trevino (b. 1978), "Poem"

TREVINO'S POEM has the energy of love and rage in art, and at art itself, with the ebullience of feeling several things at once. The word "allusion" means a kind of play, with the same root as "ludicrous." The poet's political feelings involve the serious play of alluding to— and playing with, and against, and for—ancestral, vital poems by Frank O'Hara and Wallace Stevens. The fiery attachment to those poems is partly created by anthologies, or courses, and partly by Trevino's own will: all that, too, is part of the double feeling, rising from the newspaper story about Santander Bank and from those works of art.

Poem

Santander Bank was smashed into!
I was getting nowhere with the novel & suddenly the
reader became the book & the book was burning
& you said it was reading
but reading hits you on the head
so it was really burning & the reader was
dead & I was happy for you & I had been
standing there awhile when I got your text
Santander Bank was smashed into!
there were barricades in London
there were riot girls drinking riot rosé
the party melted into the riot melted into the party
like fluid roadblocks & gangs & temporary
autonomous zones & everyone & I
& we all stopped reading

Keetje Kuipers (b. 1980), "we drive home from the lake, sand in our shoes"

INVASIVE SPECIES like kudzu, pollution like oil slicks and cellophane, insect bites, restraints like being arrested in Notasulga, Alabama: these too can comprise a stressed, confining, tender but resistant vocabulary of love.

we drive home from the lake, sand in our shoes

the dart of fish faint at our ankles, each
shuttered BBQ shack a kudzu flash

in my side mirror. Pleasure has become
the itch of a mosquito bite between

my shoulders, and your rough thumb on my thigh
a tickle gentle as turtles bobbing

in Sea-Doo oil slick and cellophane scraps.
How many years did I suffer the loves

that gave too much freedom and not enough
tenderness? Let me be like the man we

saw outside of Notasulga, hands cuffed
behind his back, cigarette in his mouth,

and you be the sheriff, leaning in close,
cupping the sweet flame to my waiting face.

DESPAIR

Dante Alighieri (1265–1321), from *Inferno*, Canto II, translated by Robert Pinsky

FEAR; WANHOPE; here "cowardice," spiritual sloth; in our modern therapeutic term "depression." Designated as the worst sin of all, because it blocks the hope for grace.

Canto II

Day was departing, and the darkening air
   Called all earth's creatures to their evening quiet
   While I alone was preparing as though for war

To struggle with my journey and with the spirit
   Of pity, which flawless memory will redraw:
   O Muses, O genius of art, O memory whose merit

Has inscribed inwardly those things I saw—
   Help me fulfill the perfection of your nature.
   I commenced: "Poet, take my measure now:

Appraise my powers before you trust me to venture
   Through that deep passage where you would be my guide.
   You write of the journey Silvius's father

Made to immortal realms although he stayed
   A mortal witness, in his corruptible body.
   That the Opponent of all evil bestowed

Such favor on him befits him, chosen for glory
   By highest heaven to be the father of Rome
   And of Rome's empire—later established Holy,

Seat of great Peter's heir. You say he came
    To that immortal world, and things he learned
    There led to the papal mantle—and triumph for him.

Later, the Chosen Vessel too went and returned,
    Carrying confirmation of that faith
    Which opens the way with salvation at its end.

But I—what cause, whose favor, could send me forth
    On such a voyage? I am no Aeneas or Paul:
    Not I nor others think me of such worth,

And therefore I have my fears of playing the fool
    To embark on such a venture. You are wise:
    You know my meaning better than I can tell."

And then, like one who unchooses his own choice
    And thinking again undoes what he has started,
    So I became: a nullifying unease

Overcame my soul on that dark slope and voided
    The undertaking I had so quickly embraced.
    "If I understand," the generous shade retorted,

"Cowardice grips your spirit—which can twist
    A man away from the noblest enterprise
    As a trick of vision startles a shying beast.

To ease your burden of fear, I will disclose
    Why I came here, and what I heard that compelled
    Me first to feel compassion for you . . .

William Langland (1330–1386), "The Glass Helmet," from *Piers Plowman*, translated by Jim Powell

ALLEGORY GOES berserk. The blundering character Life pays "gold aplenty" to Physic (more or less Medical Science), for relief from Wanhope (more or less Despair, or our modern Depression). The high-priced therapy that Life has purchased from Physic turns out to be a *glass helmet*. Crazy dilemma, crazy quest, crazy remedy, crazy image.

The Glass Helmet

Thereupon Life and his love Fortune
Begat in their glory a graceless brat,
One that wrought much woe, Sloth was his name.
Sloth waxxed wonder fast and soon was of age
And wedded one Wanhope, a wench of the stews,
Her sire an Assizer that never swore truth,
One Tom Two-Tongue, attaint at each inquest.
This Sloth waxxed sly in war and made a sling
And cast Dreadful Despair a dozen miles about.
Then for care Conscience cried upon Eld
And bade him fight and frighten off Wanhope.
And Eld took Good Hope and in haste beset him
And drove away Wanhope, and with Life he fought
And Life fled for fear to Physic for help
And besought of him succor, procured his salve
And gave gold aplenty that gladdened his heart.
And in return they gave him a glass helmet.

Fulke Greville (1554–1628),
"Down in the Depth of Mine Iniquity"

GREVILLE, WITH ambiguous charged negatives, "not" and "de-" and
"un-" and "-less," considers the interesting doctrine that even Jesus,
to endure all of the human sins, needed to feel wanhope, despairing
and forsaken for that moment on the cross, as grace is withdrawn
from him.

Down in the Depth of Mine Iniquity

Down in the depth of mine iniquity,
That ugly center of infernal spirits,
Where each sin feels her own deformity
In these peculiar torments she inherits—
    Deprived of human graces and divine,
    Even there appears this saving God of mine.

And in this fatal mirror of transgression,
Shows man as fruit of his degeneration,
The error's ugly infinite impression,
Which bears the faithless down to desperation.
    Deprived of human graces and divine,
    Even there appears this saving God of mine.

In power and truth, almighty and eternal,
Which on the sin reflects strange desolation,
With glory scourging all the spirits infernal,
And uncreated hell with unprivation—
    Deprived of human graces, not divine,
    Even there appears this saving God of mine.

For on this spiritual cross condemnëd lying
To pains infernal by eternal doom,
I see my Saviour for the same sins dying,
And from that hell I feared, to free me, come.
   Deprived of human graces, not divine,
   Thus hath his death raised up this soul of mine.

John Donne (1572–1631), "A Hymn to God the Father"

FEAR (WANHOPE) is the most dire and demanding of sins. Fear that one is hopeless is the ultimate barrier to forgiveness.

A Hymn to God the Father

I

Wilt thou forgive that sin where I begun,
   Which was my sin though it were done before?
Wilt thou forgive that sin through which I run,
   And do run still, though still I do deplore?
     When thou hast done, thou hast not done,
       For I have more.

II

Wilt thou forgive that sin by which I've won
   Others to sin, and made my sin their door?
Wilt thou forgive that sin which I did shun
   A year or two, but wallowed in a score?
     When thou hast done, thou hast not done,
       For I have more.

III

I have a sin of fear, that when I've spun
   My last thread, I shall perish on the shore;
But swear by thyself that at my death thy son
   Shall shine as he shines now, and heretofore;
     And having done that, thou hast done;
       I fear no more.

Ben Jonson (1572–1637), "An Ode to Himself"

WORLDLY, LITERARY frustration called to order by a higher, more enduring reality.

An Ode to Himself

Where dost thou careless lie
   Buried in ease and sloth?
Knowledge that sleeps doth die;
And this security,
   It is the common moth
That eats on wits and arts, and oft destroys them both.

Are all th' Aonian springs
   Dried up? Lies Thespia waste?
Doth Clarius' harp want strings,
That not a nymph now sings;
   Or droop they as disgraced,
To see their seats and bowers by chattering pies defaced?

If hence thy silence be,
   As 'tis too just a cause,
Let this thought quicken thee:
Minds that are great and free
   Should not on fortune pause;
'Tis crown enough to virtue still, her own applause.

What though the greedy fry
   Be taken with false baits
Of worded balladry,
And think it poesy?

They die with their conceits,
And only piteous scorn upon their folly waits.

Then take in hand thy lyre,
    Strike in thy proper strain,
With Japhet's line, aspire
Sol's chariot for new fire
    To give the world again;
Who aided him will thee, the issue of Jove's brain.

And since our dainty age
    Cannot endure reproof,
Make not thyself a page
To that strumpet the stage,
    But sing high and aloof,
Safe from the wolve's black jaw, and the dull ass's hoof.

Emily Dickinson (1830–1886), "The Difference Between Despair and Fear" (no. 305)

IMMOBILITY AS a violent image.

305

The difference between Despair
And Fear, is like the One
Between the instant of a Wreck
And when the Wreck has been—
The Mind is smooth—
No motion—Contented as the Eye
Upon the Forehead of a Bust—
That knows it cannot see—

Thomas Hardy (1840–1914), "The Darkling Thrush"

THE THRUSH is so excellent, so charming, that there's some temptation to neglect the poem's final three words.

The Darkling Thrush

I leant upon a coppice gate
    When Frost was spectre-gray,
And Winter's dregs made desolate
    The weakening eye of day.
The tangled bine-stems scored the sky
    Like strings of broken lyres,
And all mankind that haunted nigh
    Had sought their household fires.

The land's sharp features seemed to be
    The Century's corpse outleant,
His crypt the cloudy canopy,
    The wind his death-lament.
The ancient pulse of germ and birth
    Was shrunken hard and dry,
And every spirit upon earth
    Seemed fervourless as I.

At once a voice arose among
    The bleak twigs overhead
In a full-hearted evensong
    Of joy illimited;
An aged thrush, frail, gaunt, and small,
    In blast-beruffled plume,

Had chosen thus to fling his soul
    Upon the growing gloom.

So little cause for carolings
    Of such ecstatic sound
Was written on terrestrial things
    Afar or nigh around,
That I could think there trembled through
    His happy good-night air
Some blessed Hope, whereof he knew
    And I was unaware.

Gerard Manley Hopkins (1844–1889), "No Worst, There Is None"

AS IN the selections from Dante and Donne—there is no worst.

No Worst, There Is None

No worst, there is none. Pitched past pitch of grief,
More pangs will, schooled at forepangs, wilder wring.
Comforter, where, where is your comforting?
Mary, mother of us, where is your relief?

My cries heave, herds-long; huddle in a main, a chief-
woe, world-sorrow; on an age-old anvil wince and sing—
Then lull, then leave off. Fury had shrieked "No ling-
ering! Let me be fell: force I must be brief."

O the mind, mind has mountains; cliffs of fall
Frightful, sheer, no-man-fathomed. Hold them cheap
May who ne'er hung there. Nor does long our small
Durance deal with that steep or deep. Here! creep,
Wretch, under a comfort serves in a whirlwind: all
Life death does end and each day dies with sleep.

William Butler Yeats (1865–1939), "To a Friend Whose Work Has Come to Nothing"

"**BE SECRET** and exult." The social superiority of character and the high calling of art, without the religious component. As to exulting, maybe there's some comparison to Rita Dove's evocation of Hattie McDaniel in Hollywood (p. 171)?

To a Friend Whose Work Has Come to Nothing

Now all the truth is out,
Be secret and take defeat
From any brazen throat,
For how can you compete,
Being honour bred, with one
Who, were it proved he lies,
Were neither shamed in his own
Nor in his neighbours' eyes?
Bred to a harder thing
Than Triumph, turn away
And like a laughing string
Whereon mad fingers play
Amid a place of stone,
Be secret and exult,
Because of all things known
That is most difficult.

Theodore Roethke (1908–1963), "In a Dark Time"

A POEM that manages to redouble a feeling, almost like a summoning or a spell. Two plus two is five, or fifty, but the poet keeps on adding. (LM)

In a Dark Time

In a dark time, the eye begins to see,
I meet my shadow in the deepening shade;
I hear my echo in the echoing wood—
A lord of nature weeping to a tree.
I live between the heron and the wren,
Beasts of the hill and serpents of the den.

What's madness but nobility of soul
At odds with circumstance? The day's on fire!
I know the purity of pure despair,
My shadow pinned against a sweating wall.
That place among the rocks—is it a cave,
Or winding path? The edge is what I have.

A steady storm of correspondences!
A night flowing with birds, a ragged moon,
And in broad day the midnight come again!
A man goes far to find out what he is—
Death of the self in a long, tearless night,
All natural shapes blazing unnatural light.

Dark, dark my light, and darker my desire.
My soul, like some heat-maddened summer fly,
Keeps buzzing at the sill. Which I is *I*?
A fallen man, I climb out of my fear.
The mind enters itself, and God the mind,
And one is One, free in the tearing wind.

Elizabeth Bishop (1911–1979), "Five Flights Up"

BISHOP DID not always plan to make this the concluding poem in the last book of her lifetime, *Geography III*, but it is there, dealing with the almost-unliftable burden of memory.

Five Flights Up

Still dark.
The unknown bird sits on his usual branch.
The little dog next door barks in his sleep
inquiringly, just once.
Perhaps in his sleep, too, the bird inquires
once or twice, quavering.
Questions—if that is what they are—
answered directly, simply,
by day itself.

Enormous morning, ponderous, meticulous;
gray light streaking each bare branch,
each single twig, along one side,
making another tree, of glassy veins . . .
The bird still sits there. Now he seems to yawn.

The little black dog runs in his yard.
His owner's voice arises, stern,
"You ought to be ashamed!"
What has he done?
He bounces cheerfully up and down;
he rushes in circles in the fallen leaves.

Obviously, he has no sense of shame.
He and the bird know everything is answered,
all taken care of,
no need to ask again.
—Yesterday brought to today so lightly!
(A yesterday I find almost impossible to lift.)

John Berryman (1914–1972), "Life, Friends, Is Boring"

A POEM that could also have been included under the heading "Manic Laughter."

Life, Friends, Is Boring

Life, friends, is boring. We must not say so.
After all, the sky flashes, the great sea yearns,
we ourselves flash and yearn,
and moreover my mother told me as a boy
(repeatedly) "Ever to confess you're bored
means you have no

Inner Resources." I conclude now I have no
inner resources, because I am heavy bored.
Peoples bore me,
literature bores me, especially great literature,
Henry bores me, with his plights & gripes
as bad as achilles,

who loves people and valiant art, which bores me.
And the tranquil hills, & gin, look like a drag
and somehow a dog
has taken itself & its tail considerably away
into mountains or sea or sky, leaving
behind: me, wag.

Sylvia Plath (1932–1963), "Cut"

THE "CELEBRATION," as the poet calls it, of an occasion to show the boundless, nervous, desperate fountain of images, thrashing and leaping. As I understand it, the celebration is a perverse, ironic, triumphant denial of underlying despair.

Cut

FOR SUSAN O'NEILL ROE

What a thrill—
My thumb instead of an onion.
The top quite gone
Except for a sort of a hinge

Of skin,
A flap like a hat,
Dead white.
Then that red plush.

Little pilgrim,
The Indian's axed your scalp.
Your turkey wattle
Carpet rolls

Straight from the heart.
I step on it,
Clutching my bottle
Of pink fizz.

A celebration, this is.
Out of a gap
A million soldiers run,
Redcoats, every one.

Whose side are they on?
O my
Homunculus, I am ill.
I have taken a pill to kill

The thin
Papery feeling.
Saboteur,
Kamikaze man—

The stain on your
Gauze Ku Klux Klan
Babushka
Darkens and tarnishes and when

The balled
Pulp of your heart
Confronts its small
Mill of silence

How you jump—
Trepanned veteran,
Dirty girl,
Thumb stump.

Mark Strand (1934–2014), "Poor North"

POETRY SMILES at the gloom it invokes. Oscar Wilde with his comment about the death scene of Charles Dickens' character, exaggerates: "One must have a heart of stone to read the death of Little Nell without laughing." But art can create a feeling and its opposite, both intense.

Poor North

It is cold, the snow is deep,
the wind beats around in its cage of trees,
clouds have the look of rags torn and soiled with use,
and starlings peck at the ice.
It is north, poor north. Nothing goes right.

The man of the house has gone to work,
selling chairs and sofas in a failing store.
His wife stays home and stares from the window into the trees,
trying to recall the life she lost, though it wasn't much.
White flowers of frost build up on the glass.

It is late in the day. Brants and Canada geese are asleep
on the waters of St. Margaret's Bay.
The man and his wife are out for a walk; see how they lean
into the wind; they turn up their collars
and the small puffs of their breath are carried away.

Alan Shapiro (b. 1952), "Playground"

CIGARETTE BUTTS, condom wrappers, a playing card, a tennis ball—as with the setting, the pursuit of pleasure can supply the vocabulary of despair.

Playground

The fence can't even keep itself out now,
for years kicked in and bent up till
the bottom of it's curling
like a chain-link wave about to break
across the strip of grass
so it can wash away
or join the minor turbulence
of stubbed smokes, and condom
wrappers, and a beer can crushed
beside a queen of hearts
(thrown down in triumph
or defeat?).
                Beyond the grass
and moon glow of sand
under swings and the bony
gleaming of a jungle gym
grown colder every second
by forgetting all the busy
little heat of hands,
                the blacktop is a
black hole that has
swallowed up the chalked
hearts and initials, the foursquare
boundaries and foul lines
while beyond the fence
the fence is facing

out in the street
under the streetlight
the inside of a ripped-open
half of a tennis ball
(hit or hurled?)
is blacker than the blacktop
it is tipped toward
somewhere in which
the other half is surely lying,
tipped toward the street.
Tipped, you could say, like an ear.
You could say the silence
is the sound of one ear
listening for the other
from the bottom of an
interstellar hole.
You could say sand dunes.
Aphasic metal. The breaking
chain links of a wave. At night,
in the playground,
you could say anything.

Tracy K. Smith (b. 1972), "Solstice"

FORM, LIKE voice itself, can express the whole range of feeling. Here, the ticking machinery of the villanelle registers the thwarted, appalled response to the reported news, the grim feeling of the last five words.

Solstice

They're gassing geese outside of JFK.
Tehran will likely fill up soon with blood.
The *Times* is getting smaller day by day.

We've learned to back away from all we say
And, more or less, agree with what we should.
Whole flocks are being gassed near JFK.

So much of what we're asked is to obey—
A reflex we'd abandon if we could.
The *Times* reported 19 dead today.

They're going to make the opposition pay.
(If you're sympathetic, knock on wood.)
The geese were terrorizing JFK.

Remember how they taught you once to pray?
Eyes closed, on your knees, to any god?
Sometimes, small minds seem to take the day.

Election fraud. A migratory plague.
Less and less surprises us as odd.
We dislike what they did at JFK.
Our time is brief. We dwindle by the day.

Maggie Dietz (b. 1973), "Zoloft"

TO CHOOSE the truth of sadness, even the truth of despair, can
amount to a discovering, logic-defying joy.

Zoloft

Two weeks into the bottle of pills, I'd remember
exiting the one-hour lens grinder at Copley Square—
the same store that years later would be blown
black and blood-spattered by a backpack
bomb at the Marathon. But this was back when
terror happened elsewhere. I walked out
wearing the standard Boston graduate student
wire-rims, my first-ever glasses, and saw little people
in office tower windows working late under fluorescent
lights. File cabinets with drawer seams blossomed
wire bins, and little hands answered little black
telephones, rested receivers on bloused shoulders—
real as the tiny flushing toilets, the paneled wainscoting
and armed candelabras I gasped at as a child in
the miniatures room at the Art Institute in Chicago.

It was October and I could see the edges
of everything—where the branches had been a blur
of fire, now there were scalloped oak leaves, leathery
maple five-points plain as on the Canadian flag.
When the wind lifted the leaves the trees went pale,
then dark again, in waves. Exhaling manholes,
convenience store tiled with boxed cigarettes
and gum, the BPL's forbidding fixtures lit
to their razor tips and Trinity's windows holding
individual panes of glass between bent metal like

hosts in a monstrance. It was wonderful. It made me
horribly sad.

                                          It was the same
years later with the pills. As I walked across
the field, the usual field, to the same river, I felt
a little burst of joy when the sun cleared a cloud.
It was fricking Christmas, and I was five years old!
I laughed out loud, picked up my pace: the sun
was shining on *me*, on the trees, on the whole
damn world. It was exhilarating. And sad,
that sham. Nothing had changed. Or
I had. But who wants to be that kind of happy?
The lenses, the doses. Nothing should be that easy.

Rowan Ricardo Phillips (b. 1974), "Little Song"

THE "ALMOST" and "not quite" of the feeling, the almost arbitrary pronouns ("They close my eyes"): that partial, almost perfect unease traces the restless faltering of hope.

Little Song

Both guitars run trebly. One noodles
Over a groove. The other slushes chords.
Then they switch. It's quite an earnest affair.
They close my eyes. I close their eyes. A horn
Blares its inner air to brass. A girl shakes
Her ass. Some dude does the same. The music's
Gone moot. Who doesn't love it when the bass
Doesn't hide? When you can feel the trumpet peel
Old oil and spit from deep down the empty
Pit of a note or none or few? So don't
Give up on it yet: the scenario.
You know that it's just as tired of you
As you are of it. Still, there's much more to it
Than that. It does not not get you quite wrong.

GUILT,
SHAME,
BLAME

Anonymous, "The Cruel Mother"

A BALLAD—sung in various versions, this one making the best poem. Yes, *sung*—and as some ballads do, implying a horrendous social world surrounding the characters.

The Cruel Mother

She sat down below a thorn,
    Fine flowers in the valley;
And there she has her sweet babe born,
    And the green leaves they grow rarely.

"Smile na sae sweet, my bonnie babe,"
    Fine flowers in the valley,
"And ye smile sae sweet, ye'll smile me dead,"
    And the green leaves they grow rarely.

She's taen out her little penknife,
    Fine flowers in the valley,
And twinn'd the sweet babe o' its life,
    And the green leaves they grow rarely.

She's howket a grave by the light o' the moon,
    Fine flowers in the valley,
And there she's buried her sweet babe in,
    And the green leaves they grow rarely.

As she was going to the church,
    Fine flowers in the valley,
She saw a sweet babe in the porch,
    And the green leaves they grow rarely.

"O sweet babe, and thou were mine,"
Fine flowers in the valley,
"I wad cleed thee in the silk so fine,"
And the green leaves they grow rarely.

"O mother dear, when I was thine,
Fine flowers in the valley,
Ye did na prove to me sae kind,"
And the green leaves they grow rarely.

William Shakespeare (1564–1616), "Th' Expense of Spirit in a Waste of Shame"

A PSYCHOLOGICALLY sharp invocation of the extremes that George Herbert's "Sin" (p. 155) weighs in religious terms. "Full of blame" is an effective, exasperated anticlimax after "perjured, murderous, bloody." A similar effect structures Fulke Greville's "When all this All" (p. 85).

Th' Expense of Spirit in a Waste of Shame

Th' expense of spirit in a waste of shame
Is lust in action; and till action, lust
Is perjured, murderous, bloody, full of blame,
Savage, extreme, rude, cruel, not to trust;
Enjoyed no sooner but despisèd straight:
Past reason hunted; and no sooner had,
Past reason hated, as a swallowed bait,
On purpose laid to make the taker mad:
Mad in pursuit, and in possession so;
Had, having, and in quest to have, extreme;
A bliss in proof, and proved, a very woe;
Before, a joy proposed; behind, a dream.
    All this the world well knows; yet none knows well
    To shun the heaven that leads men to this hell.

Ben Jonson (1572–1637), "To Heaven"

HE BEGINS with a great, memorable question and works toward some wonderfully acute, alternative motives: "weariness of life" versus "love of thee."

To Heaven

Good and great God, can I not think of thee
But it must straight my melancholy be?
Is it interpreted in me disease
That, laden with my sins, I seek for ease?
Oh be thou witness, that the reins dost know
And hearts of all, if I be sad for show,
And judge me after; if I dare pretend
To ought but grace or aim at other end.
As thou art all, so be thou all to me,
First, midst, and last, converted one, and three;
My faith, my hope, my love; and in this state
My judge, my witness, and my advocate.
Where have I been this while exil'd from thee?
And whither rap'd, now thou but stoop'st to me?
Dwell, dwell here still. O, being everywhere,
How can I doubt to find thee ever here?
I know my state, both full of shame and scorn,
Conceiv'd in sin, and unto labour borne,
Standing with fear, and must with horror fall,
And destin'd unto judgment, after all.
I feel my griefs too, and there scarce is ground
Upon my flesh t' inflict another wound.
Yet dare I not complain, or wish for death
With holy Paul, lest it be thought the breath
Of discontent; or that these prayers be
For weariness of life, not love of thee.

George Herbert (1593–1633), "Sin"

COMPARE SHAKESPEARE'S "Th' Expense of Spirit in a Waste of Shame" (p. 153): in both poems, the tremendous difference between understanding and behavior.

Sin

Lord, with what care hast thou begirt us round!
   Parents first season us: then schoolmasters
   Deliver us to laws; they send us bound
To rules of reason, holy messengers,
Pulpits and Sundays, sorrow dogging sin,
   Afflictions sorted, anguish of all sizes,
   Fine nets and stratagems to catch us in,
Bibles laid open, millions of surprises,
Blessings beforehand, ties of gratefulness,
   The sound of glory ringing in our ears:
   Without, our shame; within, our consciences;
Angels and grace, eternal hopes and fears.
   Yet all these fences and their whole array
   One cunning bosom-sin blows quite away.

William Blake (1757–1827), "A Poison Tree"

BLAKE DOES not merely anticipate modern ideas about aggression and suppression. In contrast with those Latinate terms, he tells the story in vivid, specific detail.

A Poison Tree

I was angry with my friend:
I told my wrath, my wrath did end.
I was angry with my foe:
I told it not, my wrath did grow.

And I waterd it in fears,
Night & morning with my tears;
And I sunnèd it with smiles,
And with soft deceitful wiles.

And it grew both day and night,
Till it bore an apple bright.
And my foe beheld it shine,
And he knew that it was mine,

And into my garden stole,
When the night had veild the pole;
In the morning glad I see
My foe outstretchd beneath the tree.

John Clare (1793–1864), "I Am"

AN ANTHOLOGY with this title must include this poem. The third line, the last two lines of the middle stanza—heartbreaking, and guilt-ridden but somehow above merely locating the shadow of blame, in the self or in others.

I Am

I am: yet what I am none cares or knows
   My friends forsake me like a memory lost,
I am the self-consumer of my woes—
   They rise and vanish in oblivious host,
Like shadows in love's frenzied, stifled throes—
And yet I am, and live—like vapors tossed

Into the nothingness of scorn and noise,
   Into the living sea of waking dreams,
Where there is neither sense of life or joys,
   But the vast shipwreck of my life's esteems;
Even the dearest, that I love the best,
Are strange—nay, rather stranger than the rest.

I long for scenes, where man hath never trod,
   A place where woman never smiled or wept—
There to abide with my Creator, God,
   And sleep as I in childhood sweetly slept,
Untroubling, and untroubled where I lie,
The grass below   above the vaulted sky.

Thomas Hardy (1840–1914), "Channel Firing"

WRITTEN A FEW months before the beginning of what was called the Great War, a poem in which God speaks, and the dead speak and wonder if the world will ever be less insane.

Channel Firing

That night your great guns, unawares,
Shook all our coffins as we lay,
And broke the chancel window-squares,
We thought it was the Judgment-day

And sat upright. While drearisome
Arose the howl of wakened hounds:
The mouse let fall the altar-crumb,
The worms drew back into the mounds,

The glebe cow drooled. Till God called, "No;
It's gunnery practice out at sea
Just as before you went below;
The world is as it used to be:

"All nations striving strong to make
Red war yet redder. Mad as hatters
They do no more for Christés sake
Than you who are helpless in such matters.

"That this is not the judgment-hour
For some of them's a blessed thing,
For if it were they'd have to scour
Hell's floor for so much threatening. . . .

"Ha, ha. It will be warmer when
I blow the trumpet (if indeed
I ever do; for you are men,
And rest eternal sorely need)."

So down we lay again. "I wonder,
Will the world ever saner be,"
Said one, "than when He sent us under
In our indifferent century!"

And many a skeleton shook his head.
"Instead of preaching forty year,"
My neighbour Parson Thirdly said,
"I wish I had stuck to pipes and beer."

Again the guns disturbed the hour,
Roaring their readiness to avenge,
As far inland as Stourton Tower,
And Camelot, and starlit Stonehenge.

April 1914

W. S. Merwin (1927–2019), "Yesterday"

THE TITLE word calls to mind the closing lines of Elizabeth Bishop's "Five Flights Up" (p. 137), suggesting the overlapping, maybe, of "Guilt" with "Despair."

Yesterday

My friend says I was not a good son
you understand
I say yes I understand

he says I did not go
to see my parents very often you know
and I say yes I know

even when I was living in the same city he says
maybe I would go there once
a month or maybe even less
I say oh yes

he says the last time I went to see my father
I say the last time I saw my father

he says the last time I saw my father
he was asking me about my life
how I was making out and he
went into the next room
to get something to give me

oh I say
feeling again the cold
of my father's hand the last time

he says and my father turned
in the doorway and saw me
look at my wristwatch and he
said you know I would like you to stay
and talk with me

oh yes I say

but if you are busy he said
I don't want you to feel that you
have to
just because I'm here

I say nothing

he says my father
said maybe
you have important work you are doing
or maybe you should be seeing
somebody I don't want to keep you

I look out the window
my friend is older than I am
he says and I told my father it was so
and I got up and left him then
you know

though there was nowhere I had to go
and nothing I had to do

C. K. Williams (1936–2015), "The Image"

THE PHRASE "maniacally pathological" is remarkable because of the noun "readiness": a precision that creates conviction.

The Image

She began to think that jealousy was only an excuse, a front, for
      something even more rapacious,
more maniacally pathological in its readiness to sacrifice its own
      well-being for its satisfaction.
Jealousy was supposed to be a fact of love, she thought, but this was
      a compulsion, madness,
it didn't have a thing to do with love, it was perfectly autonomous,
      love was just its vehicle.
She thought: wasn't there a crazy hunger, even a delight, in how
      he'd pounced on her betrayal?
There hadn't even *been* betrayal until he'd made it so; for her, before
      that, it had been a whim,
a frivolity she'd gone to for diversion, it hadn't had anything to do
      with him, or them.
Her apologies meant nothing, though, nor her fervent promise of
      repentance, he *held* his hurt,
he cultivated, stroked it, as though that was all that kept him in rela-
      tionship with her.
He wanted her to think she'd maimed him: what was driving him
      to such barbarous vindictiveness?
She brought to mind a parasite, waiting half a lifetime for its victim
      to pass beneath its branch,
then coming to fully sentient, throbbing, famished life and without
      hesitation letting go.
It must have almost starved in him, she thinks, all those years spent
      scenting out false stimuli,

all that passive vigilance, secreting bitter enzymes of suspicion,
    ingesting its own flesh;

he must have eaten at himself, devouring his own soul until his
    chance had finally come.

But now it had and he had driven fangs in her and nothing could
    contain his terrible tenacity.

She let the vision take her further; they had perished, both of them,
    there they lay, decomposing,

one of them drained white, the other bloated, gorged, stale blood
    oozing through its carapace.

Only as a stupid little joke, she thought, would anybody watching
    dare wonder which was which.

Philip Schultz (b. 1945), "Failure"

ANOTHER POEM that declines or contradicts guilt; here, by indicting some forms of blaming. Blame itself blamed.

Failure

To pay for my father's funeral
I borrowed money from people
he already owed money to.
One called him a nobody.
No, I said, he was a failure.
You can't remember
a nobody's name, that's why
they're called nobodies.
Failures are unforgettable.
The rabbi who read a stock eulogy
about a man who didn't belong to
or believe in anything
was both a failure and a nobody.
He failed to imagine the son
and wife of the dead man
being shamed by each word.
To understand that not
believing in or belonging to
anything demanded a kind
of faith and buoyancy.
An uncle, counting on his fingers
my father's business failures—
a parking lot that raised geese,
a motel that raffled honeymoons,
a bowling alley with roving mariachis—
failed to love and honor his brother,
who showed him how to whistle

under covers, steal apples
with his right or left hand. Indeed,
my father was comical.
His watches pinched, he tripped
on his pant cuffs and snored
loudly in movies, where
his weariness overcame him
finally. He didn't believe in:
savings insurance newspapers
vegetables good or evil human
frailty history or God.
Our family avoided us,
fearing boils. I left town
but failed to get away.

Jane Kenyon (1947–1995), "Trouble with Math in a One-Room Country School"

IN ONE conventional, possibly useful distinction, shame (which the child feels here) is social while guilt (which the child declines) is theological or institutional.

Trouble with Math in a One-Room Country School

The others bent their heads and started in.
Confused, I asked my neighbor
to explain—a sturdy, bright-cheeked girl
who brought raw milk to school from her family's
herd of Holsteins. Ann had a blue bookmark,
and on it Christ revealed his beating heart.
holding the flesh back with His wounded hand.
Ann understood division. . . .

Miss Moran sprang from her monumental desk
and led me roughly through the class
without a word. My shame was radical
as she propelled me past the cloakroom
to the furnace closet, where only the boys
were put, only the older ones at that.
The door swung briskly shut.

The warmth, the gloom, the smell
of sweeping compound clinging to the broom
soothed me. I found a bucket, turned it
upside down, and sat, hugging my knees.

I hummed a theme from Haydn that I knew
from my piano lessons . . .
and hardened my heart against authority.
And then I heard her steps, her fingers
on the latch. She led me, blinking
and changed, back to the class.

Heather McHugh (b. 1948),
"Not to Be Dwelled On"

SELF-JUDGING WORDS as of an extremist, or connoisseur, of guilt.

Not to Be Dwelled On

Self-interest cropped up even there,
the day I hoisted three, instead
of the ceremonially called-for two,
spadefuls of loam on top
of the coffin of my friend.

Why shovel more than anybody else?
What did I think I'd prove? More love
(mud in her eye)? More will to work?
(Her father what, a shirker?) Christ,
what wouldn't anybody give
to get that gesture back?

She cannot die again; and I
do nothing but re-live.

Edward Hirsch (b. 1950),
"In Memoriam Paul Celan"

DESPITE THE first words of its title, this poem belongs here under the category of "Guilt" rather than "Grief." The parents of the great German-language, Romanian, Jewish poet Paul Celan (Paul Antschel) were killed by the Nazis. Celan himself was imprisoned in a work camp. He drowned himself in the Seine in 1970.

In Memoriam Paul Celan

Lay these words into the dead man's grave
next to the almonds and black cherries—
tiny skulls and flowering blood-drops, eyes,
and Thou, O bitterness that pillows his head.

Lay these words on the dead man's eyelids
like eyebrights, like medieval trumpet flowers
that will flourish, this time, in the shade.
Let the beheaded tulips glisten with rain.

Lay these words on his drowned eyelids
like coins or stars, ancillary eyes.
Canopy the swollen sky with sunspots
while thunder addresses the ground.

Syllable by syllable, clawed and handled,
the words have united in grief.
It is the ghostly hour of lamentation,
the void's turn, mournful and absolute.

Lay these words on the dead man's lips
like burning tongs, a tongue of flame.
A scouring eagle wheels and shrieks.
Let God pray to us for this man.

Rita Dove (b. 1952), "Hattie McDaniel Arrives at the Coconut Grove"

REGAL BEARING, and arriving late, as part of defiant exultation. (See Yeats, p. 134.)

Hattie McDaniel Arrives at the Coconut Grove

late, in aqua and ermine, gardenias
scaling her left sleeve in a spasm of scent,
her gloves white, her smile chastened, purse giddy
with stars and rhinestones clipped to her brilliantined hair,
on her free arm that fine Negro,
Mr. Wonderful Smith.

It's the day that isn't, February 29th,
at the end of the shortest month of the year—
and the shittiest, too, everywhere
except Hollywood, California,
where the maid can wear mink and still be a maid,
bobbing her bandaged head and cursing
the white folks under her breath as she smiles
and shoos their silly daughters
in from the night dew . . . what can she be
thinking of, striding into the ballroom
where no black face has ever showed itself
except above a serving tray?

Hi-Hat Hattie, Mama Mac, Her Haughtiness,
the "little lady" from *Showboat* whose name
Bing forgot, Beulah & Bertha & Malena
& Carrie & Violet & Cynthia & Fidelia,
one half of the Dark Barrymores—

dear Mammy we can't help but hug you crawl into
your generous lap tease you
with arch innuendo so we can feel that
much more wicked and youthful
and sleek but oh what

we forgot: the four husbands, the phantom
pregnancy, your famous parties, your celebrated
ice box cake. Your giggle above the red petticoat's rustle,
black girl and white girl walking hand in hand
down the railroad tracks
in Kansas City, six years old.
The man who advised you, now
that you were famous, to "begin eliminating"

your more "common" acquaintances
and your reply (catching him square
in the eye): "That's a good idea.
I'll start right now by eliminating you."

Is she or isn't she? Three million dishes,
a truckload of aprons and headrags later, and here
you are: poised, between husbands
and factions, no corset wide enough
to hold you in, your huge face a dark moon split
by that spontaneous smile—your trademark,
your curse. No matter, Hattie: It's a long, beautiful walk
into that flower-smothered standing ovation,
so go on
and make them wait.

Mark Halliday (b. 1959), "Milt and Sally"

SORTING THROUGH the ordinary as an encounter with the absolute.

Milt and Sally

Twenty Days After

Twenty days after my father died I threw away
all the letters between him and Sally Pierce
written in the mid-Thirties—
all that yearning and uncertainty, admiration and doubt—
the love of Milt and Sally;
she was the one he didn't marry
and in sixty-some further years he didn't forget . . .
Sally died young. Milt died very old.
Twenty days later I swam down into the files

and couldn't keep everything. Couldn't keep. Everything.

So I chucked the Sally letters, unread,
because I was not God.
God would be the Omnivorous Reader.
God might not *see* the little sparrow's fall
but if the sparrow or its mate wrote an account of it—
My Lamentable Fall From the Sky—
God would read every page;
Our Lord would savor every sentence.
And never put it back on the shelf!

My father was quite sure God didn't exist
and for most of his life he felt sure this was
a good thing, or at least extremely acceptable.
In his last two years I think he felt more

a sad irritation or that God's nonexistence is (as he would say)
a hell of a note.

Not being God, I tossed the entire yellowed bundle
and a wraith, or invisible powder of old paper,
rose from the black bag to watch me
from the ceiling of the littered posthumous apartment.
Surely the wraith could see my predicament.
Not being God, I had to be Nature.

•

God's Reading Notes

Milt was confused by too many desires,
and more romantic than he knew.
Sally was more cautious than her flamboyance implied,
and less romantic than she believed.
Milt and Sally—like their friends,
a bit overcomplicated for this green and blooded world,
but a damned good read.

Carl Phillips (b. 1959),
"After the Thunder, Before the Rain"

THE WORD "not" as a brilliant way to include and exclude, present
and temper, a much-folded, intricate set of feelings.

After the Thunder, Before the Rain

Cicadas, or locusts—by whatever name, they've at last
gone silent, like suitors outmatched by what the body can
sometimes ask for and, other times, require. You've said
what you've said. So have I. What I think I meant, though,
was not guilt, but humility: being able to see—to recognize—
a failure that belongs, finally, not so much to the dream as
to the dreamer. As if that

                   matters, now . . . Neither viciousness
nor the right kind of love, if there even is such a place. Not
abandon, but no harm, or less of it. Not at all like the mind
circling, ring upon ring—*I can't, I shouldn't, I shouldn't
have, I'll never again*—no end, no apparent ending. What I
meant was: as a suddenly wounded bird of prey, from a steep
and harder-by-the-moment-to-negotiate height descending.

Adam Day (b. 1977), "Anoosh's Obituary for Himself, to His Son"

THE EFFECTIVE, credible strangeness of what is left out and what is included, the collisions of banality and horror: all emphasize the agony.

Anoosh's Obituary for Himself, to His Son

Armaan, during the Revolution your mother
left, and I was asked to strangle a collaborator:
baggy-trousered, with a stoat-face. The house's pink wallpaper
was covered with maids and horses. Over the shower curtain
his wife's pantyhose hung. Chair-tied, sweat ran the rims
of his glasses. A lamp threw cold light, promises
were made. I'm a father. Drunk, I adjourned to the driveway
to shovel snow. There were spiderwebs of moisture
in the trees and hedges. For coffee, I used ice cream
in place of the missing milk, sick of what I knew . . .
As for your mother, Armaan, I can only say I feel better
about her infidelities when I'm well-dressed. And I am.

MANIC
LAUGHTER

John Wilmot (1647–1680), "Grecian Kindness"

ELATED RUDENESS. Mania, far from being the opposite of symmetry, sometimes exploits the methodical ebullience of it—for example, with rhyme.

Grecian Kindness

I

The utmost grace the Greeks could show
When to the Trojans they grew kinde
Was with their Armes to Let 'em goe
And leave their Ling'ring Wives behinde.
They beate the Men and burn't the Towne
Then all the Baggage was their owne.

II

There the kinde Deity of Wine
Kis't the soft Wanton God of Love:
This Clap't his wings, That prest his Vine
And their blest Powr's united move,
While each brave Greek embrac't his Punck,
Lull'd her a Sleepe and then grew Drunke.

Christopher Smart (1722–1771), from *Jubilate Agno*

HERE, THE symmetry of anaphora (like beginnings) reflects compulsion. (See Ginsberg, p. 196.) James Boswell quotes Samuel Johnson, about Smart's insanity: "His infirmities were not noxious to society. He insisted on people praying with him; and I'd as lief pray with Kit Smart as any one else."

from Jubilate Agno

For I will consider my Cat Jeoffry.
For he is the servant of the Living God, duly and daily serving him.
For at the first glance of the glory of God in the East he worships in his way.
For is this done by wreathing his body seven times round with elegant quickness.
For then he leaps up to catch the musk, which is the blessing of God upon his prayer.
For he rolls upon prank to work it in.
For having done duty and received blessing he begins to consider himself.
For this he performs in ten degrees.
For first he looks upon his forepaws to see if they are clean.
For secondly he kicks up behind to clear away there.
For thirdly he works it upon stretch with the forepaws extended.
For fourthly he sharpens his paws by wood.
For fifthly he washes himself.
For sixthly he rolls upon wash.
For seventhly he fleas himself, that he may not be interrupted upon the beat.
For eighthly he rubs himself against a post.

For ninthly he looks up for his instructions.

For tenthly he goes in quest of food.

For having considered God and himself he will consider his neighbor.

For if he meets another cat he will kiss her in kindness.

For when he takes his prey he plays with it to give it a chance.

For one mouse in seven escapes by his dallying.

For when his day's work is done his business more properly begins.

For he keeps the Lord's watch in the night against the adversary.

For he counteracts the powers of darkness by his electrical skin
    and glaring eyes.

For he counteracts the Devil, who is death, by brisking about the life.

For in his morning orisons he loves the sun and the sun loves him.

For he is of the tribe of Tiger.

For the Cherub Cat is a term of the Angel Tiger.

For he has the subtlety and hissing of a serpent, which in goodness
    he suppresses.

For he will not do destruction if he is well-fed, neither will he spit
    without provocation.

For he purrs in thankfulness when God tells him he's a good Cat.

For he is an instrument for the children to learn benevolence upon.

For every house is incomplete without him, and a blessing is
    lacking in the spirit.

For the Lord commanded Moses concerning the cats at the
    departure of the Children of Israel from Egypt.

For every family had one cat at least in the bag.

For the English Cats are the best in Europe.

For he is the cleanest in the use of his forepaws of any quadruped.

For the dexterity of his defense is an instance of the love of God to
    him exceedingly.

For he is the quickest to his mark of any creature.

For he is tenacious of his point.

For he is a mixture of gravity and waggery.

For he knows that God is his Saviour.

For there is nothing sweeter than his peace when at rest.

For there is nothing brisker than his life when in motion.

For he is of the Lord's poor, and so indeed is he called by
    benevolence perpetually—Poor Jeoffry! poor Jeoffry! the rat has
    bit thy throat.
For I bless the name of the Lord Jesus that Jeoffry is better.
For the divine spirit comes about his body to sustain it in complete
    cat.
For his tongue is exceeding pure so that it has in purity what it
    wants in music.
For he is docile and can learn certain things.
For he can sit up with gravity, which is patience upon approbation.
For he can fetch and carry, which is patience in employment.
For he can jump over a stick, which is patience upon proof positive.
For he can spraggle upon waggle at the word of command.
For he can jump from an eminence into his master's bosom.
For he can catch the cork and toss it again.
For he is hated by the hypocrite and miser.
For the former is afraid of detection.
For the latter refuses the charge.
For he camels his back to bear the first notion of business.
For he is good to think on, if a man would express himself neatly.
For he made a great figure in Egypt for his signal services.
For he killed the Icneumon rat, very pernicious by land.
For his ears are so acute that they sting again.
For from this proceeds the passing quickness of his attention.
For by stroking of him I have found out electricity.
For I perceived God's light about him both wax and fire.
For the electrical fire is the spiritual substance which God sends
    from heaven to sustain the bodies both of man and beast.
For God has blessed him in the variety of his movements.
For, though he cannot fly, he is an excellent clamberer.
For his motions upon the face of the earth are more than any other
    quadruped.
For he can tread to all the measures upon the music.
For he can swim for life.
For he can creep.

Lewis Carroll (1832–1898),
"You Are Old, Father William"

EVERY JOKE in the *Alice* books has elements of cruelty, innocence, and mania.

You Are Old, Father William

"You are old, Father William," the young man said,
   "And your hair has become very white;
And yet you incessantly stand on your head—
   Do you think, at your age, it is right?"

"In my youth," Father William replied to his son,
   "I feared it might injure the brain;
But, now that I'm perfectly sure I have none,
   Why, I do it again and again."

"You are old," said the youth, "as I mentioned before,
   And have grown most uncommonly fat;
Yet you turned a back-somersault in at the door—
   Pray, what is the reason of that?"

"In my youth," said the sage, as he shook his grey locks,
   "I kept all my limbs very supple
By the use of this ointment—one shilling the box—
   Allow me to sell you a couple?"

"You are old," said the youth, "and your jaws are too weak
   For anything tougher than suet;
Yet you finished the goose, with the bones and the beak—
   Pray, how did you manage to do it?"

"In my youth," said his father, "I took to the law,
   And argued each case with my wife;
And the muscular strength, which it gave to my jaw
   Has lasted the rest of my life."

"You are old," said the youth, "one would hardly suppose
   That your eye was as steady as ever;
Yet you balanced an eel on the end of your nose—
   What made you so awfully clever?"

"I have answered three questions, and that is enough,"
   Said his father. "Don't give yourself airs!
Do you think I can listen all day to such stuff?
   Be off, or I'll kick you down-stairs!"

Wallace Stevens (1879–1955), "The Pleasures of Merely Circulating"

IS THE arbitrary nature of the baby's nationality a nihilistic joke about reality? Or is it a scandalous joke about Mrs. Anderson's conduct? A deliberate, efficient blur, as with Lewis Carroll in the preceding poem (or Elizabeth Bishop's "Visits to St. Elizabeths" on p. 11), or in the magnetic, compulsive machinery of nursery rhymes.

The Pleasures of Merely Circulating

The garden flew round with the angel,
The angel flew round with the clouds,
And the clouds flew round and the clouds flew round
And the clouds flew round with the clouds.

Is there any secret in skulls,
The cattle skulls in the woods?
Do the drummers in black hoods
Rumble anything out of their drums?

Mrs. Anderson's Swedish baby
Might well have been German or Spanish,
Yet that things go round and again go round
Has rather a classical sound.

Marianne Moore (1887–1972), "My Apish Cousins"

THE EXHILARATION of changing the subject. And at the climax, the poet simulates the pompous jabber and jargon of literary criticism, and puts it in its place. (The place, perhaps, is an undistinguished corner of the zoo?)

My Apish Cousins

winked too much and were afraid of snakes. The zebras, supreme in
their abnormality; the elephants with their fog-colored skin
   and strictly practical appendages
      were there, the small cats; and the parakeet—
         trivial and humdrum on examination, destroying
      bark and portions of the food it could not eat.

I recall their magnificence, now not more magnificent
than it is dim. It is difficult to recall the ornament,
   speech, and precise manner of what one might
      call the minor acquaintances twenty
         years back; but I shall not forget him—that Gilgamesh among
      the hairy carnivora—that cat with the

wedge-shaped, slate-gray marks on its forelegs and the resolute tail,
astringently remarking: "They have imposed on us with their pale
   half fledged protestations, trembling about
      in inarticulate frenzy, saying
         it is not for us to understand art; finding it
      all so difficult, examining the thing

as if it were inconceivably arcanic, as symmet-
rically frigid as if it had been carved out of chrysoprase
    or marble—strict with tension, malignant
        in its power over us and deeper
            than the sea when it proffers flattery in exchange for hemp,
        rye, flax, horses, platinum, timber, and fur."

Louise Bogan (1897–1970), "Several Voices Out of a Cloud"

GET THE hell out of the way of the laurel. It is deathless, not necessarily on the approved list, and its voices may be impolite. Take that, parochial punks, nice people *et alia*. I like imagining Bogan reading this poem as her contribution to an academic or literary panel discussion.

Several Voices Out of a Cloud

Come, drunks and drug-takers; come, perverts unnerved!
Receive the laurel, given, though late, on merit; to whom
    and wherever deserved.

Parochial punks, trimmers, nice people, joiners true-blue,
Get the hell out of the way of the laurel. It is deathless
    And it isn't for you.

Stevie Smith (1902–1971), "Sunt Leones"

THE POEM deploys formalities and pomposities and clichés of differ-
ent kinds. Smith lets these trashy bits of language intersect and clash
and mock one another, creating a bladed comic focus. For exam-
ple, the dash between "if the Christians felt a little blue" and "Well
people being eaten often do": the polite "a little blue" and the bland
"Well," where two clouds imply a sharpness.

Sunt Leones

The lions who ate the Christians on the sand of the arena
By indulging native appetites played what has now been seen a
Not entirely negligible part
In consolidating at the very start
The position of the Early Christian Church.
Initiatory rites are always bloody
And the lions, it appears
From contemporary art, made a study
Of dyeing Coliseum sands a ruddy
Liturgically sacrificial hue
And if the Christians felt a little blue—
Well people being eaten often do.
Theirs was the death, and theirs the crown undying,
A state of things which must be satisfying.
My point which up to this has been obscured
Is that it was the lions who procured
By chewing up blood gristle flesh and bone
The martyrdoms on which the Church has grown.
I only write this poem because I thought it rather looked
As if the part the lions played was being overlooked.
By lions' jaws great benefits and blessings were begotten
And so our debt to Lionhood must never be forgotten.

Kenneth Koch (1925–2002), "To 'Yes'"

KOCH PRESENTS mania *for* the mind—his devotion to its rhymes and logic and associations, its literary references and knowledge of mortality, its sociability and sexuality and contradictory palaver. Beyond that, he presents mania as the quintessential quality *of* the mind. This generative frenzy is at the center of thought.

To "Yes"

You are always the member of a team,
Accompanied by a question—
If this is the way the world ends, is it really going to?
No. Are you a Buddhist? Maybe. A monsoon? Yes.
I have been delighted by you even in the basement
When asking if I could have some coal lumps and the answer was yes.
Yes to the finality of the brightness
And to the enduring qualities of the lark
She sings at heaven's gate. But is it unbolted? Bolted? Yes.
Which, though, is which? To which the answer cannot be yes
So reverse question. Pamela bending before the grate
Turns round rapidly to say Yes! I will meet you in Boston
At five after nine, if my Irishness is still working
And the global hamadryads, wood nymphs of my "yes."
But what, Pamela, what does that mean? Am I a yes
To be posed in the face of a negative alternative?
Or has the sky taken away from me its ultimate guess
About how probably everything is going to be eventually terrible
Which is something we knew all along, being modified by a yes
When what we want is obvious but has a brilliantly shining trail
Of stars. Or are those asterisks? Yes. What is at the bottom
Of the most overt question? Do we die? Yes. Does that

Always come later than now? Yes.
I love your development
From the answer to a simple query to a state of peace
That has the world by the throat. Am I lying? Yes.
Are you smiling? Yes. I'll follow you, yes? No reply.

Frank O'Hara (1926–1966), "Naphtha"

THE LAST lines of this poem could be a rubric or epigraph under the title "Manic Laughter."

Naphtha

Ah Jean Dubuffet
when you think of him
doing his military service in the Eiffel Tower
as a meteorologist
in 1922
you know how wonderful the 20th Century
can be
and the gaited Iroquois on the girders
fierce and unflinching-footed
nude as they should be
slightly empty
like a Sonia Delaunay
there is a parable of speed
somewhere behind the Indians' eyes
they invented the century with their horses
and their fragile backs
which are dark

we owe a debt to the Iroquois
and to Duke Ellington
for playing in the buildings when they are built
we don't do much ourselves
but fuck and think
of the haunting Métro
and the one who didn't show up there
while we were waiting to become part of our century
just as you can't make a hat out of steel

and still wear it
who wears hats anyway
it is our tribe's custom
to beguile

how are you feeling in ancient September
I am feeling like a truck on a wet highway
how can you
you were made in the image of god
I was not
I was made in the image of a sissy truck-driver
and Jean Dubuffet painting his cows
"with a likeness burst in the memory"
apart from love (don't say it)
I am ashamed of my century
for being so entertaining
but I have to smile

Allen Ginsberg (1926–1997), "Bop Lyrics"

A TRIBUTE to Christopher Smart (p. 180) and to the physical symmetries and kinks of words, consonants, and vowels.

Bop Lyrics

When I think of death
   I get a goofy feeling;
Then I catch my breath:
   Zero is appealing,
     Appearances are hazy.
     Smart went crazy,
     Smart went crazy.

  •

A flower in my head
   Has fallen through my eye;
Someday I'll be dead:
   I love the Lord on high,
     I wish He'd pull my daisy.
     Smart went crazy,
     Smart went crazy.

  •

I asked the lady what's a rose,
   She kicked me out of bed.
I asked the man, and so it goes,
   He hit me on the head.
     Nobody knows,
     Nobody knows,
     At least nobody's said.

•

The time I went to China
To lead the boy scout troops,
They sank my ocean liner,
And all I said was "Oops!"

•

All the doctors think I'm crazy;
The truth is really that I'm lazy:
I made visions to beguile 'em
Till they put me in th'asylum

•

I'm a pot and God's a potter,
And my head's a piece of putty.
   Ark my darkness,
   Lark my looks,
I'm so lucky to be nutty.

John Ashbery (1927–2017), "Abstentions"

"ALL OF IT as it is not": absolute rule of the imagination, in tourism, in love, in art.

Abstentions

Not the shy tourist, hopping up the salty steps of Rome—
The Piazza Venezia from a bus, the transparent emotions go by.
The old mines. Not
Just something resembling a part of it
But all of it as it is not. The voice
"Please tell me that you love me" said,
The iron monuments drift by,
The arches nailed to wood,
The caves, blind fists,
Green seaweed on the black and blue water
And the friends' precision with excitement,
"The man who sees a cloud in Schenectady
Affects someone he does not know on the other side of the globe,
   who wants him
And we shall have that rose, Dutch work apart."
Blue towers, squeals, the blind roses go by.

Therefore we have these few things.
It was a summer afternoon or night, glory was in the gondola
On the percussive honeymoon.
But he thought of the nights the ruined homes
The gold tears shed for him.

Therefore we have these white bricks.
The bride wore white . . .

He wears a white suit, carries a white newspaper and apple, his
    hands and face are white;
The clouds sneer but go sailing into the white sky.

Ishmael Reed (b. 1938), "The Author Reflects on His 35th Birthday"

REED TAKES a contagious, manic glee in, among other things, these proper nouns, with their initial caps.

The Author Reflects on His 35th Birthday

35? I have been looking forward
To you for many years now
So much so that
I feel you and I are old
Friends and so on this day, 35
I propose a toast to
Me and You
35? From this day on
I swear before the bountiful
Osiris that
If I ever
If I EVER
Try to bring out the
Best in folks again I
Want somebody to take me
Outside and kick me up and
Down the sidewalk or
Sit me in a corner with a
Funnel on my head

Make me as hard as a rock
35, like the fellow in
The story about the
Big one that got away

Let me laugh my head off
With Moby Dick as we reminisce
About them suckers who went
Down with the *Pequod*
35? I ain't been mean enough
Make me real real mean
Mean as old Marie rolling her eyes
Mean as the town Bessie sings about
"Where all the birds sing bass"

35? Make me Tennessee mean
Cobra mean
Cuckoo mean
Injun mean
Dracula mean
Beethovenian-brows mean
Miles Davis mean
Don't-offer-assistance-when
Quicksand-is-tugging-some-poor
Dope-under-mean
Pawnbroker mean
Pharaoh mean
That's it, 35
Make me Pharaoh mean
Mean as can be
Mean as the dickens
Meaner than mean

When I walk down the street
I want them to whisper
There goes Mr. Mean
"He's double mean
He even turned the skeletons
In his closet out into
The cold"

And 35?
Don't let me trust anybody
Over Reed but
Just in case
Put a tail on that
Negro too

February 22, 1973

Tony Hoagland (1953–2018), "What Narcissism Means to Me"

THESE PEOPLE embrace the mode of paying attention to one another, as an imperfect but genuine form of (largely unattainable) love. Even Sylvia's joke about Neal is attentive to him.

What Narcissism Means to Me

There's Socialism and Communism and Capitalism,
said Neal,
and there's Feminism and Hedonism,
        and there's Catholicism and Bipedalism and Consumerism,

but I think Narcissism is the system
that means the most to me;

and Sylvia said that in Neal's case
narcissism represented a heroic achievement in positive thinking.

And Ann,
who calls everybody Sweetie pie
        whether she cares for them or not,

Ann lit a cigarette and said, Only miserable people will tell you
        that love has to be deserved,

and when I heard that, a distant chime went off for me,

remembering a time when I believed
        that I could simply live without it.

Neal had grilled the corn and sliced the onions
                    into thick white disks,
                    and piled the wet green pickles
                                    up in stacks like coins
            and his chef's cap was leaning sideways like a mushroom cloud.

Then Ethan said that in his opinion,
if you're going to mess around with self-love
                    you shouldn't just rush into a relationship,

and Sylvia was weeping softly now, looking down
            into her wine cooler and potato chips,

and then the hamburgers were done, just as
the sunset in the background started
                    cutting through the charcoal clouds

exposing their insides—black,
streaked dark red,
                    like a slab of scorched, rare steak,

delicious but unhealthy,
or, depending on your perspective,
                        unhealthy but delicious,

—the way that, deep inside the misery
            of daily life,
                    love lies bleeding.

Stuart Dischell (b. 1954), "Ellipsis, Third or Fourth Dot, Depending"

THIS POEM calls to mind the expression "run with it."

Ellipsis, Third or Fourth Dot, Depending

"All my life I wanted to join the carnival.
I would be happy there upon the midway,
Tearing the heads off chickens. I know
This sounds grotesque, someone's mad ravings
Or sick bravado. How to say, I mean it only
Metaphorically. When I compare myself
I don't appear so badly. The mess I have
Made around me, which is not chicken heads
But letters, library books, shut-off notices,
Rebukes me less. I see myself as a defined
Person, one with sharp edges, a good suit
That fits and a silk shirt buttoned to the neck.
The world loves a gent. It looks at my shoes.
I wear a white scarf and I am off to the opera.
All my life I wanted to join the opera.
I would be perfect there among the painted sets,
Singing basso profundo under my cap. I could
Even play a woman there and show the crowd
Things I am capable of doing. The flowers thrown
To the footlights would enclose me like a garden.
All my life I wanted to exist in a garden.
Standing like a timepiece in the center of the lawn,
The barely perceptible movement of my shadow
Would be nonetheless significant as the hours
That revolve on my face. At night I'd be meaning-
Less to anyone but myself, or on a cloudy day.

All my life I wanted to join the clouds,
To be among them, the easily ethereal,
The ever-changing, and handsomely made. I
Would drift, congregate, vanish, roll in,
And sometimes touch the others into a day
So black the ground seems farther than the sky.
All my life I wanted to be the sky,
To carry the whole of the world inside me,
To pat my forests and deserts with satisfaction.
My God, I could be the child Sky Day,
Born on a commune to idealists, given to
Wearing black and nose rings and being twenty
For the first and only time in his/her life;
To be that shaven-headed and vital, to have
Written in paint on the wall of the city
When all my life I wanted to be that wall—
Part of the neighborhood, the block, the building:
To be seen in a rush through the express bus window
Or studied a long time in traffic. HOW MANY
DEAD, MR. PRESIDENT. NO BLOOD FOR OIL.
DANIELLE I STILL LOVE YOU. ICE RULES.
And I have wanted to be my neighborhood,
My block, my building. I have wanted
To be this city where I live, to walk down
The avenues of myself, whistling a tune
Through all the people that look like me."

Martín Espada (b. 1957), "Mad Love"

THE CATALOGUE of the unseen hurt ones is ebullient: in tribute to the father it laughs while it grieves.

Mad Love

> *No one wants to look at pictures of Puerto Ricans, Frank.*
> —*Cornell Capa*

My brother said: *They harvested his corneas.* I imagined
the tweezers lifting the corneas from my father's eyes,
delicate as the wings of butterflies mounted under glass.
I imagined the transplant, stitches finer than hair,
eyes fluttering awake to the brilliance of an open window.

This is not a horror movie. This is not Peter Lorre in *Mad Love*,
the insane and jealous surgeon grafting the hands of a killer
onto the forearms of a concert pianist, who fumbles with the keys
of the piano, flings knives with lethal aim, *Moonlight Sonata*
swept away by lust for homicide, his wife shrieking.

The blind will see like the captain of the slave ship who turned the
  ship
around, voices in the room will praise the Lord for the miracle, yet
the eyes drinking light through my father's eyes will not see the
  faces
in the lens of his camera, faces of the faceless waking in the
  darkroom:

not the tomato picker with a picket sign on his shoulder that says
Reagan Steals from the Poor and Gives to the Rich; not the fry cook

in his fedora, staring at air as if he knew he would be stomped
to death on the stoop for an empty wallet; not the poet in a beret,
grinning at the vision of shoes for all the shoeless people on the
    earth;
not the dancer hearing the piano tell her to spin and spin again;
not the gravedigger and his machete, the bandanna that keeps the
    dust
of the dead from coating his tongue; not the union organizer, spirits
floating in the smoke of his victory cigar; not the addict in rehab
    gazing
at herself like a fortune-teller gazing at the cards; not the face
    half-hidden
by the star in the Puerto Rican flag, the darkness of his dissident's
    eye.

Now that my father cannot speak, they wait their turn to testify
in his defense, witnesses to the mad love that drove him to it.

Joel Brouwer (b. 1968),
"The Library at Alexandria"

AS KATIE WILLINGHAM'S poem (p. 213) deploys the driven accelerations of thought, self-parodying yet meaningful, Joel Brouwer here arranges the related accelerations of storytelling. Narrative, too, can be parodic but meant.

The Library at Alexandria

After his wife kicked him out he began to date a Serbian librarian
whose apartment was a block from the zoo. From her bathtub
he could hear peacocks cry like cats stuck in trees. Sometimes
he heard the elephant. When the Caliph kicked the Romans out
of Egypt, he reasoned the library's scrolls either confirmed
the Koran and so were superfluous or crossed it and so
were heretical. And so and so. And so what? And so, legend says,
ordered them burned. And so, legend says, the flames heated
the city's baths for weeks. And so history gets written
to prove the legend is ridiculous. But soon the legend
replaces the history because the legend is more interesting.
When the water cooled he'd twist the squeaky silver tap
like a croupier at roulette, and the peacocks would squeak in reply.
When the librarian came home from work, she'd bring him tea
and sit on the fuzzy green toilet seat to keep him company
while November twilight slowly erased their faces. Something
barked, maybe a coyote. The librarian suggested the zoo
was itself a kind of library, but whether superfluous or heretical
she wasn't sure. She was certain the scrolls in Sarajevo's library
were sacred, just not to her. She trailed her pale fingers through
the tepid water and so his cock bobbed around like a cork.
She addressed it sometimes as Caesar and sometimes as stupid.

C. Dale Young (b. 1969), "The Halo"

WHEN A medical person named the head-immobilizing device a "halo," might there have been an element of grim comedy? Laughter and pain, laughter and dread are close relatives.

The Halo

In the paintings left to us
by the Old Masters, the halo,
a smallish cloud of light, clung
to the head, carefully framed the faces
of mere mortals made divine.

Accident? My body launched
by a car's incalculable momentum?
It ended up outside the car. I had no idea then
what it was like to lose days, to wake
and find everything had changed.

Through glass, this body went
through the glass window, the seatbelt
snapping my neck. Not the hanged man,
not a man made divine but more human.
I remember those pins buried in my skull,

the cold metal frame surrounding my head,
metal reflecting a small fire, a glow. All
was changed. In that bed, I was a locust.
I was starving. And how could I not be?
I, I . . . I am still ravenous.

Kathryn Maris (b. 1971),
"This Is a Confessional Poem"

IS THERE such a thing as comic fatalism? This poem seems to laugh at its own blend of candor and insouciance, pain and snickering, the petty and the terrible.

This Is a Confessional Poem

I am guilty of so much destruction it hardly matters
anymore. There are so many thank-you notes I never wrote
that sometimes I'm relieved by the deaths of would-be
recipients, so I can finally let go of the shame.
I was awful to someone who was attached to the phrase
"social polish," as though she'd acquire it through repetition.
I took an overdose at a child's 6th birthday party.
I was born in a country which some have called
The Big Satan. I abandoned the country for one
that is called The Little Satan. I wished ill on a woman
who has known me for years and yet never remembers
who I am—and now she's involved in a public scandal.
I have been at parties where I was boring.
I have been at parties where I was deadly boring.
I have worn the wrong clothes to sacraments, not
for lack of outfits, but for a temporary failure of taste.
I'm a terrible, terrible liar, and everything I say is full of
misrepresentation. I once knew a very sweet girl
who stabbed herself in the abdomen 7 times.
She believed she was evil and thought 7 was a holy number.
Besides that she was sane, and told me her tale
out of kindness—because guilt recognizes guilt,
the way a mother can identify her own child.
I met her in a class called "Poetry Therapy"

in which the assignment was to complete this statement:
When one door closes, another opens.
I wrote: *At the end of my suffering there was a door,*
making me guilty of both plagiarism and lack of imagination.
I was the vortex of suffering: present, future and retroactive
suffering. The girl tried to absolve me.
"Don't be Jesus," she said. "There are enough around here."
I know I should thank her if she's alive,
but I also know it's unlikely I'll rise to the task.

Jill McDonough (b. 1972), "Three a.m."

EXTREMES OF cruelty and bigotry met and engaged and effectively challenged by, of all things, laughter.

Three a.m.

Our cabdriver tells us how Somalia is better
than here because in Islam we execute murderers.
So, fewer murders. *But isn't there civil war*
there now? Aren't there a lot of murders?
Yes, but in general it's better. Not
now, but most of the time. He tells us about how
smart the system is, how it's hard to bear
false witness. We nod. We're learning a lot.
I say—once we are close to the house—I say, *What*
about us? Two women, married to each other.
Don't be offended, he says, gravely. *But a man*
with a man, a woman with a woman: it would be
a public execution. We nod. A little silence along
the Southeast Corridor. Then I say, *Yeah,*
I love my country. This makes him laugh; we all laugh.
We aren't offended, says Josey. *We love you.* Sometimes
I feel like we're proselytizing, spreading the Word of Gay.
The cab is shaking with laughter, the poor man
relieved we're not mad he sort of wants us dead.
The two of us soothing him, wanting him comfortable,
wanting him to laugh. *We love our country,*
we tell him. And Josey tips him. She tips him well.

Natalie Shapero (b. 1982), "Not Horses"

A **SKITTERY** ode to the toughness of overlooked creatures. (LM)

Not Horses

What I adore is not horses, with their modern
domestic life span of 25 years. What I adore
is a bug that lives only one day, especially if
it's a terrible day, a day of train derailment or
chemical lake or cop admits to cover-up, a day
when no one thinks of anything else, least of all
that bug. I know how it feels, born as I've been
into these rotting times, as into sin. Everybody's
busy, so distraught they forget to kill me,
and even that won't keep me alive. I share
my home not with horses, but with a little dog
who sees poorly at dusk and menaces stumps,
makes her muscle known to every statue.
I wish she could have a single day of language,
so that I might reassure her *don't be afraid—*
our whole world is dead and so can do you no harm.

Katie Willingham (b. 1988), "In Defense of Nature Poetry"

WITH "I RESIST the urge" and "But I'm wrong again" and "But I don't know / the first thing" the poem explicitly acknowledges the headlong, self-revising panic of the articulate, laughing mind.

In Defense of Nature Poetry

If you cry *get out of the woods*, the birds simply
move indoors. I say birds but we all picture
sparrows, those hearty little feather mice, fattened
on whatever their beaks will crack. In ShopRite,

they build nests of coupons, napkins, the spent tabs
of Band-Aids—I resist the urge to make a joke about
savings, nest egg—Anyway, there's no darkness
like a grocery store at night, just a sea of refrigeration cubes.

Day, darkness. Repeat, repeat. An egg laid, the little
hunger dreams of crickets miles off. And then there's
the fire escape gone fuzzy with ivy—this living thing
clinging to the inorganic. But I'm wrong again. Ivy

will climb whatever is closest, and this ladder's
made of metal, a substance found in the ground and
in the blood. As soon as it frosts, these leaves will
curl but refuse to fall. My body, too, is

governed by all kinds of laws. Every event in time just
a way of talking about space again. How much
we take up. So what's the use of a song with a birdbath, a
bank vault, a plant with metal limbs? We already have

something called the money tree. We already call
cash green. The sparrow triggers the automatic
door again—in and out—a blur of wing like a wisp
of hair, a keepsake—what we used to shut in

lockets to hold some loss. But I don't know
the first thing about survival, about treasures. I take
whatever catches the light and haul it home,
wide-eyed like a window that lets the snow right in.

NOTE

—————

I have chosen to do without some conventional items associated with anthologies, such as brief biographies of the poets or scholarly footnotes: in the age of online search engines, such information is quickly available to readers who want it.

Similarly, I have made the headnotes brief, in a spirit more of invitation than explanation. The emphasis here is immediacy, with the focus on poems and their meanings.

A small number of the headnotes are signed with a parenthetical "LM," the initials of poet and translator Laura Marris, whose careful and imaginative help have enhanced this book beyond measure.

PERMISSIONS

INDEX